RESTORATION

the Story Continues...

RESTORATION

the Story Continues...

Text by Philip Wilkinson
Photographs by Peter Ashley
Illustrations by Ptolemy Dean

ENGLISH HERITAGE

First published 2004 by English Heritage

British Library Cataloguing in Publication Data:
a CIP catalogue record for the book is available from the British Library.

English Heritage
Kemble Drive
Swindon SN2 2GZ
www.english-heritage.org.uk

Designed by Chuck Goodwin
Edited by Julia Elliott
Indexed by Lyn Greenwood

ISBN 1 85074 914 0

Printed by Bath Press C100, 7/04

Product code 50886

The BBC logo and the 'Restoration' logo are trademarks of the British Broadcasting Corporation and are used under licence.

© BBC 1996

© BBC 2003

This book is published to accompany the television series *Restoration: the Story Continues…*, which is produced by Endemol UK Productions, part of Endemol UK plc.
Executive producers: Nikki Cheetham and Annette Clarke
Series producer: Katie Boyd

www.bbc.co.uk/restoration

The picture on the title page shows the 1895 Wesleyan chapel at Brotherhood Bar, south of Spalding in Lincolnshire. Derelict and forgotten, this building, small but typical of this part of Eastern England, was recently demolished. *Restoration* aims to protect such buildings, and to stop their needless destruction.

CONTENTS

CLARENCE HOUSE

Last year, like many people up and down the country, I watched with great interest the unfolding of the first series of *Restoration* which culminated in people voting for the Victoria Baths, Manchester, to be the recipient of funds to help restore its Turkish Baths. Having met the volunteers involved with that particular project, as well as many hundreds of other enthusiasts engaged in similar projects throughout the country, I never cease to be amazed by their passion and determination for their heritage; these people, from all walks of life, show just how much people care about the old familiar buildings around them, the buildings with character and charm which they recognise form the backdrop to their communities – something that was recognised, too, by the many millions of viewers and by those who voted for their favourite buildings.

Restoration reveals, I believe, the value and significance of the great architecture that is such an important part of this country's inheritance – an architectural heritage that encompasses not only our internationally famous buildings, but also the buildings that make up the "spirit of place" of our individual neighbourhoods. It is this pride in our local heritage that comes through so strongly in the series. I believe we are truly nourished by our surroundings, never more so than at a time when such ugliness abounds, and that we feel starved when buildings that are important to us fall into disuse, become derelict or are destroyed.

This book, accompanying the second series, features not only the range of buildings being championed in this series, but also shows what has happened to the buildings featured in 2003 in the first series. It is hugely heartening that several of them have found rescuers and now have an assured future.

Restoration also makes it clear that, although rewarding, the challenges of restoring and conserving historic buildings are always considerable. This book, published by English Heritage, shows how you can tackle some of those challenges. The individual stories of the buildings covered here are truly inspiring – not just because they show what can be done to save our architectural heritage, but because they show how important these places are in supporting communities and giving us a sense of belonging and identity.

It is my hope that *Restoration* will also help inspire a new generation of young people to learn the building crafts and skills that were used to create these beautiful buildings. These are traditional skills which the nation can ill-afford to lose if we are to continue to protect and maintain what is so valuable to us all and, most importantly, to begin to create a really worthwhile heritage for our descendants.

Acknowledgements

Philip Wilkinson would like to thank: the team at Endemol for taking time out of a busy production schedule to answer questions and supply information about the buildings featured in the series; May Blair, Anna Chalcraft, and Alastair Glen for sharing the fruits of their research; Sheila Watson and Sugra Zaman for their support; Zoë Brooks for good humour and good sense; Val Horsler and Rob Richardson for taking the project on, keeping us on track, and drawing the threads together; Julia Elliott for her editing and knowledge; Chuck Goodwin for the speed and elegance of his design; Ptolemy Dean for allowing his remarkable and sensitive illustrations to appear in this book; and Peter Ashley for photographs that embody the spirit of every building.

In addition the author would like to thank the following individuals – members of Building Preservation Trusts, staff of local authorities and heritage organisations, and other custodians – for discussing and supplying information about the buildings that mean so much to them, and now to me:

Giles Harvey (Sherborne House) Adam Wilkinson (Castle House) Martin Eddy (South Caradon Mine) Barry Gray (Severndroog Castle) Anna Chalcraft and Michael Snodin (Strawberry Hill) Michael Goulden and Hilary Collins (Llanfyllin Union Workhouse) Howard Stone (Celynen Workingmen's Institute and Memorial Hall) Glen Johnson (Cardigan Castle) Alastair Glen (Portencross Castle) Steve Callaghan (Hall of Clestrain) Hugh Jones (Knockando Wool Mill) Trevor Geary (Armagh Gaol) May Blair (Lock-keeper's cottage) Pauline Ross (The Playhouse) Clare Dykes (Sheffield Manor Lodge) Graham Bell (Gayle Mill) Henry Thompson (Lion Salt Works) Gillian Crawley (Newstead Abbey) Mary Wain (Bawdsey Radar Station) Rob Morris (Old Grammar School and Saracen's Head).

Thanks also to the following for supplying information about the progress that has been made on the buildings featured in the first series of *Restoration*:

Peter Howard (Poltimore House) Les Owen (Arnos Vale Cemetery) Heather Goddard (Whitfield Tabernacle) Christine Rogers (Wilton's Music Hall) Phillip Smart (Darnley Mausoleum) Keith Moss (Broomfield House) Ramsay Milne (Glen o'Dee Sanitorium) John Smith (Easthouse Croft) Tom Cane (Kinloch Castle) Judith Bowers (Britannia Music Hall) Chris Lewis (Mavisbank House) Alan Lodge (Nairn's Linoleum Factory) William Wilkins (Llanelly House) Sean Wood (Vaynol Old Hall) Liz Donnan (Crescent Arts Centre) Stuart Graham (Lissan House) Celia Fergusson (Herdmans Mills) Richard Evans (Wentworth) Lisa McCleod (Harperley Prisoner-of-War Camp) Graham Bell (Ravensworth Castle) Richard McCoy (Brackenhill Tower) Richard Bramley (Bank Hall) Jennifer Freeman (Bethesda Chapel) Elizabeth Perkins (Newman Brothers) Jonathan Catton (Coalhouse Fort) Byron Hahn (Moulton Windmill).

Endemol would like to thank: Katie Boyd, Susanne Curran, Nikki Cheetham, Annette Clarke, Griff Rhys Jones, Marianne Sühr, Ptolemy Dean, Giles Worsley; Andrea Miller, Audrey Baird, Richard Downes; Paul Coueslant, Jonathan Barker, Kate Scholefield, Tom Stubberfield, Rob Pendlebury; Andrew Thompson, Paul Overton, Sarah Barclay; Susan King, Val Campbell, Monica Patel, Sandie Paterson, Emma Derrick, Morgan Holt, Lucy Bowen. The BBC would also like to thank Jane Gilmartin, Tom Hodgkinson, and Sandy Raffan.

Peter Ashley would like to thank the following, who so helped to smooth the progression of his epic journey: Brian Alderson, Christine Beckwith, Lucy Bland, Lucy Bowen, Anna Chalcraft, Christine at King's Norton, Emma Derrick, Clare Dykes, Julia Elliott, Rupert Farnsworth, Andrew Fielding, Andrew Gadd, Alastair Glen, Chuck Goodwin, Dr Barry Gray, Richard and Jane Gregory, Giles Harvey, Val Horsler, Clare Jamison, Glen Johnson, Hugh Jones, Sue Lewis, Mark Lucas, Aidan Mallon, Niall McCaughan, Alex McLaren, Wynne Morris, Victoria Petterson-Turner, Biff Raven-Hill, Rob Richardson, Kit Routledge, Michael Snodin, Howard Stone, and, last alphabetically but foremost in much understanding, Philip Wilkinson.

PREFACE

We at English Heritage are passionate about protecting and conserving the buildings that are the physical evidence of our past. They are an integral and vital part of the environment, wherever we live, and their loss damages us all. This is why we maintain our annual *Buildings at Risk Register*, which lists all the Grade I and II* listed buildings and structural monuments in England that are at risk through neglect and decay or vulnerable to becoming so. That list is, sadly, rather a long one; but it is excellent that programmes like *Restoration* are highlighting the problem and leading to projects that result in major buildings being rescued, conserved, and reused.

We were an integral part of the first *Restoration* series, as we are of the second. And we are delighted to seal our collaboration with the 2004 project by publishing the book of the series, in association with Endemol and the BBC.

The 2003 series generated enormous publicity for the endangered buildings it featured, and led to rescue plans for several of them – not just the winner. It also led to wide public debate on the principles and practices of restoration, and the challenges faced by the dedicated and brave people who take up the cudgels on behalf of a much-loved, but neglected, local landmark. This book, in addition to telling the stories of the buildings in the 2004 series, focuses on those principles and challenges, and hopes to further the debate and to involve more people in this vital work.

Dr Simon Thurley
CHIEF EXECUTIVE, ENGLISH HERITAGE

Sherborne House

Castle House

South Caradon Mine

Strawberry Hill

Severndroog Castle

Old Grammar School and Saracen's Head

Bawdsey Radar Station

Manor Lodge

Gayle Mill

Celynen Workingmen's Institute

Portencross Castle

Hall of Clestrain

RESTORATION

Archbishop's Palace

INTRODUCTION

The BBC2 series *Restoration* was first screened during August and September 2003, with resounding success. Impressive ratings saw viewers' votes generating over £500,000 for the Restoration Fund, to which the Heritage Lottery Fund added a further £3 million. Manchester's Victoria Baths, the building that was announced as the winner after a fiercely fought vote during the final of the series, is in line to receive this money. Meanwhile, partly as a result of the publicity and support garnered by the programmes, many of the other buildings in the first series are moving closer towards restoration.

Now the *Restoration* team is back with a second series. Griff Rhys Jones explores another twenty-one buildings from all over Britain, while architect Ptolemy Dean and building surveyor Marianne Sühr give their expert opinions, unpicking the history of each building, explaining how it came to be at risk, and outlining plans for the future. This book follows their

Newstead Abbey

Lion Salt Works

Cardigan Castle

Llanfyllin Union Workhouse

Knockando Wool Mill

Lock-keeper's cottage

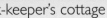

Armagh Gaol

The Playhouse

stories, and gives progress reports on many of the buildings from the last series, explaining how local custodians and enthusiasts are carrying on the good work of campaigning and fund-raising to try to save the precious heritage in their care.

As before, selecting the buildings has been difficult. But the programme-makers take good advice, making their choice in collaboration with English Heritage, Historic Scotland, Cadw (Welsh Historic Monuments), and the Environment and Heritage Service (Northern Ireland). The emphasis is on buildings that are or will be in public or charitable hands, where plans for a sustainable new use are under way and where public access will be possible when restoration is complete. There is a broad geographical spread, from Orkney to Cornwall. And the range of buildings is vast, from glamorous country houses to industrial buildings that have played a vital part in the history both of their local region and of the entire nation.

The variety of buildings is one of the things that keeps surprising people about *Restoration*, and about our architectural heritage as a whole. The restoration candidates are often little known outside their own areas – indeed, even nearby, people are frequently surprised that there is such a gem in their own backyard. And they are even more amazed when the cameras take them close to the building and they learn from Marianne and Ptolemy how tiny details – perhaps a fragment of moulding, the size of the bricks, or a join in the masonry – can provide vital clues about the structure's age and history.

For many people, beginning to understand buildings in this way is a first step towards getting involved in restoration themselves. This may take the form simply of joining one of the national heritage bodies, such as English Heritage, Historic Scotland, or the National Trust, visiting more of their properties and helping to fund their work through the membership fee. It may mean getting involved with one of the restoration candidate buildings by offering to help with funding or campaigning. Another route is to join one of the courses run by the Society for the Protection of Ancient Buildings or one of the other architectural societies, perhaps even learning one of the building crafts. Ultimately, it could even mean taking on your own building for restoration. This book gives some advice on where to find information about this (see page 224).

Bawdsey Radar Station

Draw a building and you will see it more clearly, understand it more fully. Ptolemy Dean drew many of the restoration candidates while on location for the TV series. Some of the results, together with Ptolemy's comments on the buildings, appear on pages 128–143. A few more of his drawings are reproduced here.

Lion Salt Works

Those who have already become more involved have discovered that the restoration of any historic building is a complex and fascinating process. It involves close study of the building, the weighing up of a host of questions and problems, and the use of specialised craft skills from masonry to metalwork. But, precisely because there are so many factors and so many skills involved, because buildings are large and complex structures to work on, and because of the need to get it right, the restoration process cannot be rushed.

It all begins with research – finding out as much as possible about the building so that its restoration respects its history and does not destroy what it seeks to preserve. All kinds of expert advisers, from building surveyors to paint analysts, may need to be brought in before plans can be made. And then there is funding. Building work is costly, skilled restoration work especially so. A relatively modest project can cost a million pounds, for which one would have to raise nearly £3,000 every day for a year. As a result, many projects apply for funding to the grant-giving bodies, such as the Heritage Lottery Fund, who will require detailed plans – often including an assurance that the building will be viable, that it will pay its way after restoration is complete, so that there will not be further requests for money to prop it up in a few years' time. In addition, there will be requirements that the public will have access to the restored building and probably that various kinds of interpretation and explanation are provided so that visitors can learn about the building's history and importance. If public money is to be spent, the public should benefit from the project. Finally, the work itself has to be done carefully and painstakingly, using traditional methods with the minimum disruption to the existing fabric of the building.

Severndroog Castle

So no one should be disappointed if candidates from the first series of *Restoration* are not yet restored. Most have made substantial progress and updates describing recent developments are given in the relevant chapters of this book. All these buildings have a wealth of enthusiastic local advocates, their ranks increased as a result of the publicity from the series. They are working hard for the buildings in their care, and, with their determination and with public support, they will get there in the end.

Portencross Castle

RESTORATION – A DYNAMIC PROCESS

The last two hundred years have seen fundamental changes in the philosophies, processes, and practicalities of restoration. And attitudes change subtly with the changing needs of every building that is restored. This chapter looks at some of these changes, examining how views have developed over time, what kinds of issues restorers have to face, and how these result in a variety of approaches to the immense range of buildings that make up our architectural heritage. We begin in the late eighteenth century, when many of Britain's ancient buildings were facing a crisis.

The search for perfection

Many of the great British cathedrals contain fabric that dates back to just after the Norman Conquest. By the late eighteenth century, a number of these buildings were falling into disrepair. Falling literally, in the case of Hereford Cathedral where, on Easter Monday 1786, the medieval west tower crashed to the ground. The cathedral authorities called in James Wyatt, one of the most versatile architects of the time, to undertake a thorough restoration.

Like most English cathedrals, Hereford had evolved over hundreds of years and different parts were built in different styles. Both the round arches and thick walls of the Normans and the pointed arches and windows of the later Gothic period were visible. Wyatt took the opportunity to remodel Hereford, sweeping away the Norman upper levels of the nave and rebuilding these, and the cathedral's damaged west end, in the Gothic style. In doing this he was seeking to unify the appearance of the cathedral, especially the exterior, so that from the outside it gave the impression that it was entirely Gothic.

Hereford Cathedral

Wyatt carried out similar 'improving' restorations at a number of other English cathedrals. At Salisbury he removed a free-standing bell tower, demolished two fifteenth-century chapels, moved the choir screen, replaced surviving medieval stained glass with clear glazing, limewashed over the ancient paint on the vaults, and took away the gravestones from outside the building. Some of these alterations, such as the demolition of the chapels, took the cathedral closer to its original form for, unlike Hereford, Salisbury was built almost completely in one style, the Early English Gothic of the thirteenth century. Others were exercises in tidying, smoothing over the fabric to bring it to a state of neatness and purity that was quite alien to the thirteenth century.

At Durham, too, Wyatt smoothed out the fabric – by actually taking a thick layer off the decayed and roughened outside walls. He also planned to demolish the Galilee, a late-Norman chapel that protrudes from the west front of the cathedral, but this work was not carried out. Nevertheless, Wyatt had done enough here and elsewhere to earn himself the nickname 'the destroyer'.

Wyatt's case was extreme, but the principle underlying his work, that of restoring a mythical former perfection to a building, was

A raised platform is used for high shots and to get the camera closer to the upper levels of the buildings in *Restoration*. This shoot, at Portencross Castle, brought the camera – and viewers – much closer to the structure's high walls than is normally possible.

not unusual. Similar ideas guided most church restorers in the nineteenth century. Few old cathedrals or parish churches escaped restoration in that century, and most of the new work was carried out in the Victorian version of fourteenth-century Decorated Gothic, the style which was then deemed the most appropriate for religious buildings.

Many Victorian architects constructed whole careers out of church building and church restoration. Most famous of all was Sir George Gilbert Scott, who worked on a variety of churches and cathedrals, including Chester, Chichester, Ely, Lichfield, Ripon, and Salisbury. In contrast to Wyatt, Scott took a more conservative attitude to restoration. At Salisbury, for example, he removed some of the additions made by Wyatt and restored some of the colour that Wyatt had obliterated from the vaulting. And Scott's work was often vital. At some sites, if he had not intervened, centuries-old buildings would simply have collapsed.

Even so, the scraping away of the surfaces of ancient masonry and the repeat prescription of 'fourteenth-century Gothic' were too much for some. The critic John Ruskin, in his 1849 work Seven Lamps of Architecture, spoke of the impossibility of copying an ancient surface that has eroded away and decried the 'brute hardness' of newly restored masonry. But the real crisis did not come until the 1870s, when Scott's plans to restore the Norman abbey at Tewkesbury in Gloucestershire were made public. William Morris fired off a letter to The Athenaeum, which appeared on 5 March 1877:

> My eye just now caught the word 'restoration' in the morning paper and, on looking closer, I saw that this time it is nothing less than the minster of Tewkesbury that is to be destroyed by Sir Gilbert Scott. Is it altogether too late to do something to save it – and whatever else beautiful or historical is left to us on the sites of the ancient buildings we were once so famous for?

By the time Morris wrote his letter, Scott's work at Tewkesbury was already under way. He was too late to stop Scott. But Morris's protest bore fruit in another way. The Society for the Protection of Ancient Buildings (SPAB) was formed, with Morris as its first Secretary, to save old buildings from decay, damage, demolition, and insensitive restoration.

Georgian houses, like this terrace in Bridgwater, were not valued highly by the Victorians. The Georgian Group was founded to preserve such buildings and to educate people about how to care for them. Now they are prized – both for their contribution to our towns and for the spacious, light accommodation they provide.

SPAB's Manifesto, written in 1877 and still guiding the work of the Society, argues against the Victorian wish to 'bring back a building to the best time of its history' and encourages those in charge of ancient buildings,

> to stave off decay by daily care, to prop a perilous wall or mend a leaky roof by such means as are obviously meant for support or covering, and show no pretence of other art, and otherwise to resist all tampering with either the fabric or ornament of the building as it stands; if it has become inconvenient for its present use, to raise another building rather than alter or enlarge the old one; in fine to treat our ancient buildings as monuments of a bygone art, created by bygone manners, that modern art cannot meddle with without destroying.

This policy, advocating skilful repair over destructive restoration, marked a sea change in attitudes to old buildings. Because of the involvement of architects such as Philip Webb and W. R. Lethaby in SPAB it became accepted amongst many in the architectural profession. It is still immensely influential today.

Protecting our heritage

In the years since SPAB was founded, a host of different organisations have appeared, all in different ways supporting the ideal of preserving our heritage of buildings. One of the earliest was the National Trust, founded in 1895 to preserve places of historic

interest and natural beauty. The Trust now owns and protects, and opens to the public, some two hundred historic houses and around fifty industrial sites. It also owns hundreds of smaller properties, many let to tenants and many historically important. With this vast portfolio of property, millions of members, and thousands of volunteers, the Trust has become a national institution – so much so that many people do not realise that it is a charity, and quite independent of government. The Ancient Monuments Society is another organisation with a broad remit. The Society supports all sorts of historic buildings through such activities as giving advice, running courses and producing publications, and working within the planning system to protect buildings at risk.

Other heritage organisations have been established to support buildings of specific periods. Morris and his contemporaries were interested mainly in the buildings of the medieval era – roughly, those built before about 1500 – and those built under the Tudors and Stuarts. Georgian buildings still seemed modern to the Victorians, and had few supporters until the 1930s, when the Georgian Group was founded. By the mid-twentieth century, a number of architectural historians and other enthusiasts were putting the case for the architecture of the Victorian period, something that had been deeply unfashionable, partly indeed as a result of the restoration activities of men like Scott. In 1958 the Victorian Society was founded, at the instigation of John Betjeman, 'to make sure that the best Victorian buildings and their contents do not disappear before their merits are generally appreciated'. By 1979, the architecture

For years art deco buildings like the Ovaltine factory at Kings Langley, Hertfordshire, were ignored by conservationists. Many were demolished, but a few remain as evidence of the flair of the designers of the 1920s and 1930s. The Twentieth Century Society campaigns on behalf of others that have been less well preserved.

of the 1930s had been brought under the watchful eye of the Thirties Society, which later became the Twentieth Century Society. Bodies such as these provide information, run courses, campaign on behalf of buildings at risk, and are consulted when proposals are put forward to alter or demolish notable buildings of their period.

Then there are the groups that specialise in buildings of a particular type – such as the Cinema Theatre Association, the Association for Industrial Archaeology, and the Churches Conservation Trust. Working in a variety of different ways, these organisations offer support ranging from campaigning to custodianship for specific groups of buildings.

Other organisations take a still more active role in building preservation. The Landmark Trust, for example, was formed in 1965 as an independent building preservation charity. It rescues historic buildings from neglect, restores them, and lets them as holiday accommodation, using the income from letting to fund the buildings' upkeep. More recently, in 1997, the Prince of Wales's Phoenix Trust was launched, to repair and find new uses for major historic buildings at risk. It works in partnership with other bodies – from national organisations such as English Heritage to local communities – and has developed schemes for important industrial, hospital, military, and naval buildings both providing and implementing viable solutions for often large and problematic old structures. Our built environment is benefiting enormously as a result.

Official measures

All these groups and organisations, large and small, represent a huge body of interest in the buildings we have inherited, its participants ranging from specialist scholars and building conser-vationists to those with no specialist knowledge who simply want to visit or appreciate what previous generations have left behind. In addition to this popular movement there are also official measures, enacted by government, to protect our heritage. The most important of these began, like the wider conservation movement, in the late nineteenth century with the first Ancient Monuments Act (1882), which scheduled sixty-eight monuments. Another early step on this legal ladder was the appointment in 1908 of the Royal Commissions on Historical

Monuments for England, Wales, and Scotland, instigating a programme of making inventories and records of historical monuments. This work was buttressed by the foundation of the National Buildings Record (later the National Monuments Record) in 1941. Still more support for old buildings was provided by a series of Town and Country Planning Acts from the 1940s onwards, requiring lists of buildings of architectural and historical interest to be drawn up and giving listed buildings special protection.

English Heritage was created by another Act of Parliament in 1983. It is the government's statutory adviser on the historic environment and acts to conserve and enhance that environment, broaden public access to the heritage, and increase people's understanding of the past. It does this in many ways, often involving partnership with other bodies, from government departments to private companies. Its work ranges

English Heritage cares for hundreds of historic sites, including a large number of ruined buildings. This one is Moreton Corbet Castle, Shropshire, where the ruins of a medieval castle stand beside the remains of an Elizabethan mansion.

from looking after an impressive collection of ancient monuments to providing advice on planning decisions which affect the historic environment, and from scholarly research to involvement in the Restoration series. Similar work is done north of the border by Historic Scotland and in Wales by Cadw.

One task performed by English Heritage is the maintenance of a register of buildings at risk in England. These are all notable buildings, structures of historical or architectural importance, and all are under threat in some way – neglect, vandalism, or sheer lack of money has meant that they are suffering from decay, dilapidation, or even total collapse. When the first series of Restoration was screened, there were almost 1,500 buildings on English Heritage's register. There are a similar number on the register today, and the problem is showing no sign of disappearing. In spite of the work of all the amenity societies, national heritage organisations, and others, there is still a huge backlog of work to be done.

Why preserve?

At first glance, many buildings at risk appear to be lost causes. Once the roof has gone and damp, vegetation, and vandals invade a building's structure, it rapidly turns into a ruin. For some people, pouring huge resources into restoring a building like this is a waste – they argue that it would be better to employ a good modern architect to build a new structure, suitable to the needs of today. In view of such opinions, it is worth asking why we should spend money on preserving the buildings of the past.

On the simplest level of all, people like old buildings – they appeal to our need for the beautiful and the picturesque in our lives. But they go much deeper than this. Old buildings form strong links with the past. They tell us much about our history – to historians and archaeologists they are precious documents, unlocking information about the life, art, aspirations, and technology of the people who built them and used them.

Restoration allows those studying an old building still greater access to this historical evidence. When a structure is damaged and repaired, layers often get peeled away. Missing or damaged decoration reveals details of hidden structural elements, or the

When English Heritage acquired Wigmore Castle, Herefordshire, in 1996, they decided to adopt a very gentle, non-interventionist approach to the site. Instead of excavating to reveal buried walls, laying concrete paths, and tidying everything up, they consolidated the walls and left the castle as a romantic ruin. They also employed an ecologist to look after the site's wildlife – even the plants growing on the wall tops. The result is an object lesson in 'organic' conservation.

marks left when a building has been altered, or other unsuspected details from past eras. In the first series of Restoration, for example, Marianne and Ptolemy were able to prise away 1960s hardboard and reveal unique eighteenth-century panelling and oil paintings at Llanelly House, to trace forgotten early fireplaces at Bank Hall, and to point out early timber and brickwork at Broomfield House. In the current series, they find traces of vanished walls at the Hall of Clestrain, peer beneath elaborate Gothic decoration at Strawberry Hill, and marvel at the stonework in buildings like Portencross Castle. As the restoration process begins, such details can be recorded, to build up a picture of the history of the building – a picture which in turn informs the restorers as they take difficult decisions about how to carry out their task.

Buildings from the past play a special role in the identity and pride of an area. Restore an old building, repair its broken roof or its cracked walls, or replace its peeling decoration, and you can give an immense uplift to a neighbourhood. First and foremost, this uplift is psychological – people feel better about their area if the most important buildings are cared for and can be shown off to admiring visitors. But the improvement can also be economic. Get a restoration project right, and it can bring in visitors, businesses, and jobs, acting as a powerful catalyst for local regeneration.

In addition, there is the environmental benefit. There is an enormous amount of energy involved in producing a building and it makes sense to make the best use of it. For example, it takes the energy equivalent of a barrel of oil to make just eight bricks. By the same token, it takes energy to restore or conserve a building. But the implication is clear. It is at the very least worth assessing a building as an environmental resource before demolishing it.

What to preserve

So the arguments for preservation are powerful and varied. But which buildings should we preserve? Those who are interested in conservation, from pressure groups to government departments, speak of buildings of architectural or historical significance. But how do we define the significance of a building? This was the question in the mind of the inspectors who set out to make Britain's first inventories of listed buildings during the 1940s. They were armed with a set of instructions defining the types of buildings that they should consider. These instructions are fascinating, because they throw light on how we value old buildings – and on the kinds of buildings chosen as restoration candidates in the BBC series.

The first category of building for listing is perhaps the most obvious of all – buildings that are clearly outstanding works of art in their own right. Many are large buildings, big country houses like Blenheim Palace or cathedrals such as St Paul's, and represent the work of a single architect. They do not have to be big, however – many are small and compact, such as Sir Christopher Wren's Church of St Stephen, in Walbrook, London, which is just as clearly an artistic masterpiece as the nearby St Paul's. In the current series, Strawberry Hill is a notable representative of this type of building, an outstanding example of the work of a creative genius, Horace Walpole, which became hugely influential on later designers and architects.

Next come buildings that, while not outstanding masterpieces, exemplify a particular style of design. Many British towns have the occasional house that stands out as a particularly fine example of Georgian or Victorian architecture. The architect may be unknown, or the house may have been built by a local builder using the designs in a pattern book, but the result is

At Vaynol Old Hall, a restoration candidate from the previous series, layers of decoration have been removed to reveal the underlying structure.

Buildings of national importance, like St Paul's Cathedral, are among the most obvious candidates for preservation. They also influence today's planners and builders. In the case of St Paul's, the recent Millennium Bridge over the Thames makes an impressive approach and enhances the view of the dome from south of the river.

These two buildings are typical of their period. This brick Georgian house (left), part of the Geffrye Museum in east London, is like many that enhance the townscape in this part of the city. The railway station at Wellingborough, Northamptonshire (right), is a shining example of the Victorian builder's art, from imitation Norman windows to ornate carved bargeboards at the eaves.

something typically of its period. The Hall of Clestrain, a Georgian house on Orkney, is a good example amongst the restoration candidates.

Then there are buildings that have grown organically over many years or even centuries. Countless British buildings have been added to in this way and the result can be an architectural hotchpotch. But it can still have a special appeal. As the instructions to the building investigators puts it, such a building can form, 'an outstanding composition of fragmentary beauties welded together by time and good fortune'. Thousands of parish churches fall into this category, many exhibiting work from the Norman, Gothic, Georgian, and Victorian periods. Houses, too, often grow over time. Even an apparently Georgian building, like restoration candidate Sherborne House, can reveal a much earlier Tudor core.

Freaks and follies make up another category of building that is often worth preserving. These are unique and often bizarre

buildings that stand slightly to one side of British architectural tradition. They include sham castles built to enhance the view from country houses, water towers designed like the bell towers of Italian cathedrals, and the pagoda in Kew Gardens. Severndroog Castle is the restoration candidate that falls into this category.

Some sites are important because of what they show us about the lives of former generations. These are often industrial sites and such buildings, especially those that mark a key phase in the industrial revolution or the later history of British industry, are increasingly recognised as candidates for preservation. Restoration candidates such as the South Caradon copper mine or Gayle Mill are worth preserving not because of their looks – although such sites sometimes have a beauty of their own – but because they form a part of the historical development of an area and were central to the lives of its inhabitants. They form unique windows on the past – and for locals represent a tangible link with ancestors who worked there. So such buildings are just as much a part of our history as grand palaces and

Built in the sixteenth century and altered in the seventeenth, the Bell Inn at Stilton, Cambridgeshire, is one of those buildings that has grown over the years, acquiring interest and beauty with age. It is also worth preserving for its place in culinary history – it is the original home of Stilton cheese.

cathedrals, and visitor numbers at many industrial heritage sites show that the public recognises this.

The historical importance of a building may be more specific. Links to famous people of the past give an old building an added dimension and many of the homes of the great figures in our history have already been preserved and opened to the public. Visitors to London can see the houses of a variety of historical figures, from John Keats to Sigmund Freud. Among the restoration candidates, Portencross Castle has links with the first Stuart king, Robert II, while Sherborne House regularly played host to both Thackeray and Dickens, so the historical associations stretch from north to south.

Finally there are buildings that are worthy of preservation because they form part of a notable group. They may be part of a famous historical settlement, such as the Wiltshire villages of

Whissendine Windmill, Rutland, looks good from the outside, but its real glory is within, where there is a complete functioning set of machinery. For this is a working mill, producing flour for sale, a shining example of how restoration and conservation can bring old industries back to life.

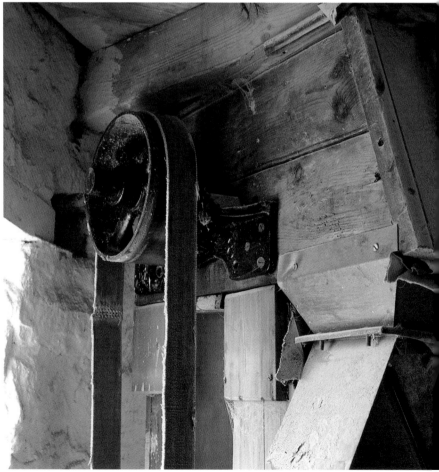

Lacock or Castle Combe. Or they may be components of one of Britain's contributions to the story of town planning, such as Regency Cheltenham or, on a still grander scale, Georgian Edinburgh. An individual terraced house in Cheltenham or Edinburgh may not be an architectural masterpiece, but its place in the whole scheme of things is vital.

From this selection of types of structure one can see that the preservation and restoration of historic buildings is a subject of endless diversity. If, when they think of restoration, people think first of all of great country houses and cathedrals, they need to be aware of the significance of all sorts of other structures – industrial buildings, buildings in unlikely materials, buildings that have been unjustly neglected. A concrete house from the mid-nineteenth century, an imitation castle, a gaol, or a miners' institute – all are worthy restoration candidates and all have fascinating stories to tell.

One of the most remarkable groups of late nineteenth-century buildings is at Port Sunlight, Cheshire, the model village built for workers at William Lever's Sunlight Soap factory. Each must be preserved to protect the integrity of the whole.

Some constant guidelines ...

Old buildings are almost infinitely varied, but even among this diversity, conservation experts have been able to set down some universal guidelines about how to treat them. Above all, regular maintenance and repair are always preferable to restoration. With maintenance of the appropriate kind, using materials such as lime mortars that allow the fabric to shift and 'breathe', old buildings can survive for generations without major restoration. Providing the will and the money are available, structures can be kept off the buildings at risk registers.

But all too often the will or the money are not available and major repair or restoration becomes the only way to save the building. In such cases, new building work should be carried out in ways that do not destroy the building's fabric. It should respect the irregularities that are often a feature of early buildings. It should not prevent further repairs in the future. And it should be reversible, so that it can be redone or altered without damaging the original parts of the structure. Any new fittings should be made so that they fit the old fabric, rather than adapting the old to fit the new.

Perhaps the most important guiding principle of all is that any new work on an old structure should come after a careful study of the building. This sort of study should cover every aspect, including architecture, structure, the changes that have been made to the building during its life, and the history of its use. And this study should be ongoing – more facts may be revealed as work progresses and these should be added to the study so that further work can be informed by all the available research.

... and some issues for debate

These guidelines leave many further decisions to be made about how to work on an old building, and some of these are the subject of heated debate amongst practitioners. One issue concerns the extent to which new repairs should be visible and identifiable as new. To take an example from a different discipline, when art restorers fill in missing areas in a fresco, some try to make their new colours look as closely as possible like the work of the original artist, while others prefer the more 'honest'

The stone gatehouse at Donnington Castle, Berkshire, was long ago patched in brick. Modern conservators face a dilemma – whether to make repairs as obvious as this or to go for a more discreet approach.

St Mary's Church at Islington, Norfolk, is partly ruined. It is in the care of the Churches Conservation Trust.

approach of marking the new work, perhaps with faint cross-hatching, to indicate clearly that it is the work of a later hand.

A similar dilemma can face a restorer repairing a wall. Should one use recycled bricks or treat stone so that it looks old? Or should one use new but otherwise similar materials, so that anyone looking at the building can see at once that a repair has been made? The first approach might provide more visual unity to the façade of a building, but many conservators today would prefer the second approach as more 'honest'. The environmentally conscious often prefer recycled materials, but bricks that have been removed from a wall and cleaned often look strikingly different from those that have remained in situ. And recycling raises another issue – the architectural salvage industry can be unscrupulous about the sources of the goods it sells.

There are many other issues that face anyone conserving or restoring old buildings. They include which methods should be used to clean masonry, whether modern materials may be substituted for costly traditional ones, and whether sometimes it is necessary to change the design of a feature to make a building more durable. Such issues show that restoration is not a simple business, for there are difficult decisions to be made throughout a project, and good advice, careful planning, and

St Albans Cathedral is one of many that underwent drastic restoration in the Victorian period. Today's custodians respect the whole building – even the Victorian additions.

Llanfyllin Union Workhouse is one of the featured buildings in *Restoration*. Any work done on the structure will involve finding a new, viable use.

thorough study of the building need to inform the process from beginning to end.

Another issue affects buildings that have been altered over time. How many of the later alterations is it advisable to remove? The answer to this question depends on a clear vision of the building's significance. Sometimes it is quite easy to decide. Take the case of an eighteenth-century town house that has survived almost intact, except for some alterations made mainly to the ground floor when the building was converted to a shop in the 1960s. The 1960s changes are limited to concealing Georgian panelling and other decorative details behind plasterboard and the addition of shop fittings. It would not be difficult to decide to remove the undistinguished 1960s fittings and reveal and conserve the Georgian details beneath.

A very different case would be a medieval parish church that has been altered and adapted many times since it was first built by the Normans in the early twelfth century. A thirteenth-century chancel, fifteenth-century aisles and tower, and Georgian pews have been added. There is also a Victorian vestry. Each of these extensions and additions has lent something new to the building, which has become just such an example of a harmonious blend of architectural periods and styles imagined in the instructions to investigators quoted above. Each part of the building needs to be conserved and no part merits demolition.

All too often, though, old buildings present a more problematic case. One person's irrelevant Victorian extension is another's example of the work of an unjustly neglected architect. And additions that seem peripheral to a building's main importance may have their own story to tell about the history of the way the place was used, its occupants, or hidden details of construction. So in assessing a building, it is a good idea to think back to the much-abused cathedral restorations of the nineteenth century, to which William Morris and John Ruskin objected so strongly. From a twenty-first-century perspective, Wyatt's west front at Hereford Cathedral or that of the equally notorious restorer Lord Grimthorpe at St Albans are now an integral part of each building's history. We would no more think of demolishing them than we would the medieval masonry behind them. They are part of the story these cathedrals have to tell us – and a reminder that the Victorians too were faced with a problem, for without the work of Wyatt, Scott, and Grimthorpe, many of our churches might simply have fallen down.

The restoration candidates themselves present a vast variety of different buildings, demanding diverse approaches. In some cases, in order to save a building, some alterations might be necessary to permit a change of use. A structure like Llanfyllin Union Workhouse is a case in point. It cannot be restored to its original function – workhouses no longer exist – but it is a solid, well-built structure with a range of interior spaces that could be adapted for business or community use with relative ease. Since many of the original interior features have in any case been stripped away, it makes sense to restore the exterior and make sensitive adaptations inside to give the building a new, viable role.

Sometimes, by contrast, a building is important because its original contents are preserved and it is still used for its original purpose. Knockando Wool Mill in Morayshire, for example, is full of nineteenth-century machinery for textile manufacture, all in working order and in regular use. Clearly the priority here is to conserve the building so that the mill can continue working, as well as restoring other notable features, such as the nineteenth-century water wheel.

These are two examples of the many different approaches that are adopted by those involved in caring for buildings at risk in Britain today. There are many others — perhaps as many as there are buildings – but all involve balancing the varied requirements of funders, users, visitors, and conservationists. But slowly and surely, approaches like these are taking structures off the buildings at risk registers and giving them new, sustainable futures – and we can all benefit from that.

Knockando Wool Mill, Morayshire, another restoration candidate, is still used for textile production. The aim of restoration is both to preserve the building and to allow spinning and weaving to continue.

THE SOUTH WEST

Sherborne House SHERBORNE

Castle House BRIDGWATER

South Caradon Mine BODMIN MOOR

Most people have an affectionate image of the South West. They think of it as a place of rugged coasts and narrow lanes, of warm sun and cream teas. In spite of cheap international air travel, it is still an area where many British people take their holidays. But *Restoration* looks beyond the popular image of Cornish fishing villages and the thatched cottages of Devon to seek a very different South West, though one still rooted in the very stone of the area.

Stone structures have been part of the landscape of the region for thousands of years. The South West has more prehistoric monuments than any other British region, and they are incredibly wide-ranging. Most famous of all are the great stone circles, Stonehenge and Avebury. But just as impressive in their way are the remains of small Bronze Age villages like Grimspound on Dartmoor – some twenty-four hut circles enclosed within a stone wall about 150 metres across.

So there is an ancient tradition of building in the South West, and this is often related to an interesting use of local resources – from the stone used by the prehistoric builders at Grimspound to the tin and copper extracted by Cornwall's generations of miners. The area's three restoration candidates reflect this, demonstrating between them how a mixture of local resources and local skills can come together to produce remarkable buildings. The three candidates from the South West could not be anywhere else.

One of the buildings, Sherborne House in Dorset, was the creation of a local architect and builder from a family who worked widely in the county. The founder of this dynasty was Thomas Bastard, a joiner and builder from Blandford Forum. Little is known about his buildings, many of which probably disappeared in a fire that engulfed Blandford in 1731. But by the time he died in 1720 he had six sons, several of whom were successful carpenters, architects, and builders. John, William, Benjamin, and Joseph Bastard worked widely, rebuilding Blandford after the fire and combining the skills of carpentry, masonry, and architecture with considerable flair. Sherborne House shows Benjamin's skill to perfection.

The other domestic candidate in this region is the mid-nineteenth-century Castle House in Bridgwater. This structure is a monument to a very different builder, John Board, who used the building as a showcase for the material he manufactured and championed – concrete. Board stood out from the crowd in his enthusiasm for concrete. Bridgwater was and is a town known especially for its bricks and tiles, and Board wanted to do something different. In its way Castle House is just as notable an achievement as Bridgwater's beautiful Georgian brick terraces, a

The crumbling structure of Castle House in Bridgwater, a house built largely of concrete in the mid-nineteenth century, is hidden under protective scaffolding.

At South Caradon in Cornwall, copper mining created a landscape of contrasts, etching tracks and depressions of rocky greyness on Bodmin Moor.

virtuoso work in a material that most people in the mid-nineteenth century thought of as new and unusual.

Finally, the copper mine at South Caradon tells a typically Cornish story, for mining is as central to Cornish history as fishing or tourism. South Caradon is a memorial to the people who discovered its copper deposits and started a veritable mineral rush in the area in the late 1830s. But it is also a reminder of countless others who worked there, risking their lives in order to extract metal that was in demand all over the world. If it has created a bizarre and surprising landscape for the region, it could not be more closely linked to the history of the area.

These three sites are notable achievements of the South West in many ways. But one thing that unites them is that they were built by people who knew the meaning of risk. Concrete was a commercial risk for John Board, a new material for house building that did not catch on in his lifetime. Mining was a risk for everyone at South Caradon — many lost their lives or sustained terrible injuries. Even the Bastards of Blandford knew about the risk of fire, for they had seen their town and their work burn to the ground. In spite of such perils, all these buildings have survived. Their custodians know that helping them through the next century will not be easy either, but will be a worthwhile way to honour the buildings' visionary creators.

The Georgian elegance of Sherborne House is shielded by a garden wall and the gentle shade of surrounding trees.

Sherborne House

Good proportions, classical details, generous windows to let in plenty of light – features like these are typical of Georgian domestic architecture and Sherborne House displays them all. Indeed, it has been described as the finest house in the Dorset town from which it takes its name. Looking at its elegant entrance front, concealed behind a tall brick wall, it is easy to see why. And this well-proportioned façade hides other treasures – fine Georgian interiors and unique murals. In addition, this is a house with evocative memories. It has been home to many tenants, including a famous actor and a girls' school.

Now the house is an arts centre, playing a key part in the cultural life of Sherborne and the South West. As Giles Harvey, who is closely involved with the arts centre and the plans for the restoration, explained, 'The arts centre supplies an important local need – there are no exhibition spaces of this sort of size nearby. But we also have a national role because of the importance of some of the artists whose work we show.' These range from the internationally known British artist Gavin Turk to artists who were members of the Bloomsbury Group, whose work has been shown in a major exhibition. The artistic director of the centre also acts as artist in residence, and produces work that responds to the history of the house and the memories that surround it.

The story of this Georgian house began in 1720, when it was built for Henry Seymour Portman, the second son of a baronet, who became well known as a soldier. Portman only used his house for a few years because he died in 1727, and for much of the next two hundred years the house was let to a succession of tenants before becoming a girls' school between 1931 and 1992.

Probably the most famous of the tenants was the Victorian actor William Charles Macready. Macready became an important figure in the cultural life of Sherborne, founding a literary institute which met at the house. Among the friends who visited the actor here were the novelists William Thackeray and Charles Dickens. A regular visitor, Dickens came here at a turning point in his life – the start of his first reading tour. On these tours, which continued for the rest of his life,

The quoins, keystones, and other details are just as important on the side elevation (left) as on the more prominent entrance front.

The front is full of careful details (below). The way in which the centre portion is brought forward slightly adds interest to the façade and draws the eye to the doorway and central windows, which are topped with pediments.

Dickens gave dramatic readings of his works, taking all the parts himself and moving audiences to tears with his performances. The year 2004 marks the 150th anniversary of the first tour, and a special re-enactment of his reading of *A Christmas Carol* is due to take place at Sherborne.

Because the house was let to tenants, Sherborne's owners did little to alter the fabric. So it remains a well-preserved example of the architecture of its period — and one that retains parts of an earlier Tudor house that Portman absorbed into his own. As Giles Harvey explained, 'The Tudor wing, which is to the left of the 1720 house, currently contains the gallery. This structure was originally a substantial three-storey Tudor house, but was partly demolished when the 1720 house was built. The architect's idea was probably that it should supply the domestic offices – the kitchen, buttery, and so on – for the new house. Since then the Tudor wing has been altered by the Victorians. So now it contains some nineteenth-century windows, but there are also still several original Tudor windows, and carved Tudor roof bosses can also be seen.'

But it is the eighteenth-century house that is under the greatest threat. The failing roof and parapet gutters are letting in water, and there is already damage to the upper floors as a result. The public cannot be allowed access to these parts of the house because of the deteriorating state of the fabric. And some of these upper rooms are important in themselves – the second-floor rooms contain original panelling and chimney pieces and in the eighteenth century had rich hangings. The fear is that the water will penetrate further, destroying unique decorations and details. Sherborne House is in need of restoration – and urgently.

From the front, Sherborne looks like a typical larger house of the early eighteenth century. And all the details emphasise its quality. There are rows of sash windows, each set off with a

A detail of the door surround shows the complexity of the moulding that separates the pilaster from its base.

moulded surround. There are larger corner stones, or quoins, which seem to frame the whole building. The centre of the façade is topped with a shallow triangular pediment. Beneath the pediment, the wall is brought forward slightly to give the building greater interest and to lead the eye to the doorway, which also has a miniature pediment above. All these details show the care that was taken with the building's design and mark it as typical of its period.

The architect responsible for this carefully detailed front was from a family of builders well known in Dorset, the Bastards. Two Bastards, John and William, rebuilt much of Blandford Forum to make it one of the West Country's finest Georgian towns. Their brother, Benjamin, was the designer of Sherborne House.

Benjamin Bastard took just as much care with the interior, and many of his touches remain inside the house. Most magnificent of all the interior spaces is the staircase. The stair itself is impressive. Its high-quality carving and marquetry work show the Bastards' background – they were joiners and cabinet-makers as well as builders. But more magnificent still are the paintings on the walls and ceiling, which are the work of the most famous mural-painter of the period, Sir James Thornhill. The Portman family had a connection with Thornhill, because

No effort was spared on the doorway (below left), with its curved pediment and uprights finely carved with classical mouldings. The lead-topped pediment has protected these details well and the stonework is still in good condition.

Deep-cut blocks, called quoins (below), set off the corners of the building.

The red and blue in the upper part of Thornhill's staircase mural still glow (opposite), but the painting is deteriorating and in urgent need of restoration.

The fine woodwork of the banister (left) is a tribute to the tradition of carpentry in the Bastard family.

Caught in the sunlight (below), Thornhill's painted decoration still creates the effect of stonework with gilded details.

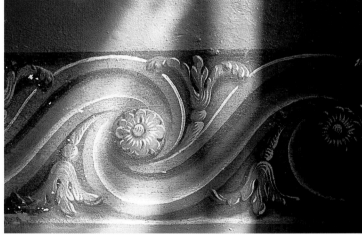

they were patrons of All Souls College, Oxford, where Thornhill had redecorated the chapel. The painter was also rebuilding his own family home, some ten miles to the east of Sherborne, and so was a natural choice to work on the new Portman house.

In the fashion of the times, Thornhill drew his subject matter from ancient Greek mythology, depicting a story concerning Artemis, the goddess of hunting. Artemis was angered when Oeneus, ruler of Calydon, did not make a sacrifice to her after the harvest. So she sent a giant boar to ravage his fields. The boar killed several of Oeneus's men, but was finally killed by his son, Meleager. The story of Meleager and the boar is shown on the walls around the staircase, while Artemis looks down from the ceiling.

An actor prepares to bring the house to life in one of *Restoration's* reconstruction scenes.

The result is a magnificent painting, and, as Giles Harvey pointed out, this is one of the few places in the South West where the public can see this artist's work, because many of his surviving paintings are in large buildings in the South East. But the murals are now showing their age. Both the subtle monochrome of the lower levels, designed to imitate the effect of carved marble, and the colours above are dirty and in places are beginning to flake. Restoration of the painting is vital and the money for this has been raised, but work cannot go ahead until the roof above has been made watertight.

The staircase alone would make Sherborne House worth restoring, but many of the other rooms have outstanding Georgian fixtures and fittings. Chimney pieces, panelling, and fine doorcases, together with fittings such as locks, doorknobs, and hinges, abound in many rooms. Many of the windows have their original sashes and shutters, and some retain their Georgian glazing, with all the charming irregularities that give it a 'life' quite lacking in modern plate glass. The place is a treasure-house of Georgian details.

Of course, in almost three hundred years of use, many decorative details have disappeared. But here the restorers will be helped by a rare survival. The 1726 inventory of the house, written by Benjamin Bastard himself, provides a full account of how each room was furnished and also describes the colour scheme used in most rooms. This document would enable many of the rooms to be recreated almost exactly as they were in the 1720s, and the restorers plan to use its listings, along with analyses of the layers of paint in each room, to choose their colours. The inventory also provides invaluable evidence of how life was lived at Sherborne – it even includes Portman's silver chamber pot.

So the plan is to restore many of Sherborne's Georgian features, but also to keep the place running as an arts centre. The centre has an agreement with the estate of renowned sculptor Dame Elizabeth Frink, who lived at nearby Woolland. Under this agreement, many of her works will be displayed at the house, some in indoor galleries and others in a specially created sculpture garden. In the house itself, the downstairs rooms, where most of the panelling and other Georgian details survive, will be restored to reflect the design of the house in 1720. Upstairs, where gallery space is planned, many Georgian details will be retained, although it is also planned to install sympathetic gallery lighting.

So the future looks bright for Sherborne House. The building's importance is clear and its use is already well established. As Giles Harvey summed up, 'We have a proven track record of putting on events that attract large audiences, and we're confident that, if we can get funding for the restoration, we can give the house a sustainable future. We have a great past and we are confident that we can give the house a great future.'

Giles Harvey contemplates the grounds through one of the house's beautifully made sash windows.

Castle House

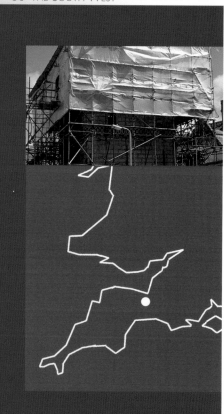

Sometimes the closer you look at a street, the more surprises it yields. Castle House, in the middle of the Somerset town of Bridgwater, is just such a building. Bridgwater is above all a town of brick. It is known for streets of elegant, brick-built Georgian and early Victorian houses – and, built on clay, it was also, from the eighteenth century onwards, the centre of Somerset's brick and tile industry. In 1851, however, John Board, the owner of a cement-manufacturing company, decided to show what could be done with the material he made. So he built Castle House out of concrete.

It seems a bizarre choice in 1851, when street after street of new houses was going up in red brick and when stone was the material of choice for many buildings, such as churches, where a more monumental appearance was required. Adam Wilkinson of SAVE, the organisation championing the house through its SAVE Trust, explained: 'It was intended as a sort of show home for concrete, to show examples of what could – and couldn't – be done with this material.' Board used part of the building as his office, so that clients could come and see how versatile his products were.

The mid-nineteenth century seems early for a concrete house, but the material had already been used widely, especially in large engineering projects, and had a long history. The Romans had used concrete extensively, and although Roman knowledge of concrete was lost in the Middle Ages, the material was revived in the eighteenth century, when types of concrete were developed that would set hard in water, for use in structures such as harbours and lighthouses. The first concrete bridge was built in 1816 in Souillac, France. In 1825, concrete was used in the construction of the Erie Canal in North America. The first house to be made completely of concrete was put up in 1835, in Swanscombe, Kent. And in the 1840s, Prince Albert incorporated much precast concrete work into the new royal house at Osborne, on the Isle of Wight.

By this time, two major advances were making concrete more widely useful. The first was the invention in 1811 of Portland cement. This material, devised by British engineer Joseph Aspdin, is made by burning a controlled mixture of clay and limestone.

The resulting clinker is ground to a powder and gypsum is added to the mixture to control the speed at which the material sets when mixed with water. Hard and strong, with setting characteristics that can be controlled, Portland cement was soon being used widely in the construction industry.

Although strong under compression, concrete is weak in tension, and engineers devised ways of making it stronger by combining it with iron bars or wires. This was also an early nineteenth-century development, with many different engineers devising different reinforcement systems. Thomas Telford used iron bars in the concrete abutments of the Menai Bridge in 1825, and in the 1850s a number of different patents were filed for various types of concrete reinforcement.

The exterior is a showcase of what can be done with concrete. The massive masonry, imitating rusticated blocks, the window frame and dripstone with its moulded heads, the statue in the niche, and the band of interlaced circles – all are examples of concrete effects more usually seen in stone.

A close-up shows that some of the details are rather shallowly moulded. A stone-carver might have cut them more crisply and deeply, but they are still effective.

The year 1851, as well as being when Castle House was built, was also the year of the Great Exhibition at Crystal Palace. Osborne House was awarded a medal at the exhibition, and one of the wonders on display was Portland cement. This was the material Board used for Castle House – or Portland Castle as it was originally called. In the mid-century it seemed that the time was ripe for the market for concrete to boom.

Unlike many modern architects, Victorian builders like Board did not appreciate concrete for its raw, unadorned appearance. What impressed Board was how you could use it to imitate the highest-status building material of the time – stone. Above all, because concrete could be poured into moulds, you could make it into virtually any shape, and Castle House is a showcase for the use of poured concrete. From the outside this is immediately apparent. The front is highly ornate, designed in the style of a Tudor gatehouse. On the lower levels, precast concrete facing panels cover walls of brick. Above, the walls are made of solid concrete blocks, designed to imitate rustication, the style of masonry in which stone blocks are separated by deeply cut joints to give a pleasing pattern of flat surfaces and grooves, and of light and shade. Above and below the first floor are friezes made of precast concrete panels supported on concrete corbels. Still higher, the mock battlements are brick-built but covered in cement render.

The roof, covered with pantiles, looks more traditional and more in keeping with the pattern of local building. But even this is an innovative structure, held up in part by curious trusses made of bricks, as if, having banished brickwork from the walls of his house, Board was determined to show how this local material could be made to serve modern ends.

Inside the house the concrete theme persists, and there are many concrete details. Staircases, handrails, and window frames were all prefabricated at Board's works. The skirting is in concrete, and the material was used for interior floors. Early visitors would have been amazed that such details, which would normally have been made with skilled and costly handwork in timber or stone, could be mass-produced in a cheap, easily available, mouldable material. Board must have hoped that builders and clients alike, enthused with Castle House, would come flocking with orders for concrete corbels, concrete stair treads, indeed whole houses of concrete.

So, together with his son-in-law (a piano and organ builder), Board set up his office in the new house, which also held residential accommodation. In a few places, concrete caught on. At the same time as Castle House was built, the Medina Cement Company of the Isle of Wight was building simple, plain concrete houses at East Cowes Park. Other individual concrete houses went up, such as the late nineteenth-century 'The Mount' at Burnham-on-Sea, which was built by Board's grandson using construction techniques similar to those showcased at Castle House.

Treads for the spiral staircase, produced to a uniform size and shape, were easy components to make in concrete.

Eroded by the weather and defaced by paint and bird droppings (above), some of the carvings on the exterior are in urgent need of conservation.

Other details still retain their crispness and elegance – one can imagine John Board's pride in what he had produced.

But, for the most part, the concrete fever that Board hoped for did not materialise. The nation-wide building boom of the late nineteenth century, in which millions of houses were constructed to accommodate rapidly growing city populations, was conducted mainly in brick, with elements such as floors and stairs in traditional wood and roofs of slate. Concrete only became common as a material for house building in the twentieth century, and Board's exciting vision was decades ahead of its time.

Meanwhile, Castle House went into decline. In the 1940s it was split into several flats and its fabric began to deteriorate. Some of the problems started as a result of the innovative structure. Pieces of wood were let into the concrete to enable door frames and other fittings to be attached. These pieces of wood are now rotting and are destined to fail. More seriously still, the structure started to crack as a result of subsidence and there were attacks by arsonists and vandals. The apparently sturdy concrete walls could hardly stand without the aid of a supportive network of scaffolding. The house was finally bought by a developer who hoped to convert it to a nursing home.

'The Mount' at Burnham-on-Sea was demolished in 1983, and an application to demolish Castle House was also expected.

This became a spur for campaigners to take on the cause of the Bridgwater house and here, demolition was averted. The building was eventually handed over to the SAVE Trust, which is now looking after Castle House and working towards its restoration. The Trust is well aware of the size of the problem. The threatened structure needs to be stabilised and the whole building needs a new roof. When this work is done, the interior will be converted into three flats that will be let by a local housing association.

Adam Wilkinson is conscious of the benefit such a restoration could make to the town: 'We would like this project to be a great benefit to Bridgwater, a super town within easy commuting distance of Bristol that has gone through a period of decline. Restoring Castle House would be beneficial in two ways. It would make a huge improvement to the townscape in an area that was partially cleared in the past to provide service yards for local shops. It would also create some much needed housing in the centre of the town – and perhaps encourage others to provide more.' So saving Castle House would beyond doubt be a benefit to Bridgwater.

It would also be a national benefit, because this is a unique structure with a complex place in the history of building in Britain. Castle House is in one way a building ahead of its time, a concrete house when such structures were rare, which looks forward to the use of precast and reinforced concrete in the twentieth century and celebrates the diverse uses of the material, from decorative friezes to floor panels. But it is also a building very much of the nineteenth century. The Victorians were fascinated by new materials, by inventions, by engineering feats. They had great architects, but their real heroes were engineers, men like Isambard Kingdom Brunel, who tamed technology and opened up new transport routes and new ways of life. But at the same time the Victorians were conservative in the arts, embracing revivalist styles of architecture, and it is no accident that Castle House is mock-Tudor in appearance. So restoring this building would preserve a national treasure, too, one which sums up the Victorian age and looks forward to the modern era.

South Caradon Mine

They say that if you look into a hole in the ground anywhere in the world, you are likely to find a Cornishman at the bottom of it. Mining was a way of life in Cornwall for centuries. The Romans bought tin from Cornwall and in the nineteenth and early twentieth centuries Cornish mining was still thriving. The last tin mine, South Crofty near Redruth, closed in 1998. The area is still famous for its tin-mining heritage, but in some places there are deposits of lead and copper, the metal that made the owners of South Caradon Mine rich.

The mine was opened in 1838, right at the start of the Victorian period, and closed in 1890. What is left are a number of industrial buildings together with an extraordinary, almost alien, landscape that surprises every visitor. Countryside Officer Martin Eddy described the approach across Bodmin Moor. 'There's a touch of mystery about the place. There is a narrow entrance down a lane, and it's impossible to see what is coming up ahead. Then suddenly the view opens up and you see this amazing man-made landscape – mounds of soil and rocks, a vast open wound that somehow never seems to heal.'

It is an evocative landscape, scooped out of the moor. Engine houses with tall chimneys, some with Gothic details, puncture the skyline. Great heaps of 'stuff', the rock left over when the ore was extracted, now covered with grass, loom large. Shafts, covered with metal gratings or masked by trees, have become dumping grounds for old furniture.

The story of South Caradon began in the nineteenth century. The first people to search the area for mineral deposits were local miner James Clymo, his brother Peter, and members of a local farming family, the Kittows. Following and extending a passage into the rock, they had found ore by 1836, but they could not persuade anyone to invest in the mine. So they decided to finance the venture themselves and were soon glad they did. Shares they had offered at £5 each were soon worth £2,000.

The 1840s and 1850s were the boom years for the mine. Producing almost 4,000 tonnes of ore per year, the place was alive with activity and there were six hundred people working on the site, including women and children as young as eight

The gaunt remains of the mine buildings still make a powerful silhouette above the moorland.

years old. Elsewhere in the county mines were declining in the face of cheap Malaysian tin and copper from South Africa and South America. But South Caradon, with its high production, was able to keep going. Soon the place was famous all over Cornwall, and several new mines were named 'Caradon' in the hope of attracting investment. But none of these matched the success of South Caradon itself.

The impact on the local area was enormous. The population increased dramatically as workers flooded in. Housing was overstretched and overcrowding became the norm. Roads around the mine were jammed with traffic bringing in coal and taking away ore. The local tracks, previously used only by farm carts, could not take the strain and soon a railway was built to the foot of the mine.

The next twenty years saw continued high production, with up to 6,000 tonnes of ore per year being extracted. But the profits dropped with falling copper prices. By the 1880s, attempts to refinance the mine, to extend the workings, and to combine operations with other local mines had proved to be a

series of false starts. In 1890 working ended and the mine closed for good. Many of the miners left the area, some emigrating to find jobs in mines in other parts of the world.

They left behind a number of buildings, including several evocative engine houses. The engine houses, with their adjoining boiler houses and chimneys, contained the great beam engines that pumped water out of the mines. Some have all but disappeared, most are ruined, and one or two still stand more or less intact, with great stones to support the engines.

Rectangular engine houses and tall, round chimneys are the most common building remains at South Caradon. In their ruined state they are typical of the Cornish industrial landscape of the last two centuries.

A buttress supported the wall of an engine house, to help the structure withstand the constant pounding of the great engine within.

The granite walls of the mine buildings are hard as nails – there is little sign of damage from the weather, even in this exposed position.

One such, Jope's Engine House, still stands to its full height, but is badly damaged by ivy growth.

For some, these remains are a scar on the beloved scenery of Bodmin Moor. But this place is a vital part of Cornwall's history, as Martin Eddy was keen to point out. 'This heritage is part of the people's psyche in Cornwall,' he said, recalling that Cornish people are proud of the mining history that dominated so many of their ancestors' lives. Many were involved in the tin mining for which Cornwall is most famous, but locals are equally aware of South Caradon's history of copper mining. For some the place has the added resonance of a memorial. A number of miners were killed at their work, and for their descendants the site is a moving monument to them and their dangerous jobs.

Another thing that makes the place special are the stories that attach to its history. Martin Eddy remembered one tale about the site's original owners. 'The story goes that part of the site was owned by two old ladies who sold the land to a lawyer. They then got wind of the fact that there was copper there and quickly went back to the purchaser. They claimed that they still had a sentimental attachment to the place and wanted to buy it back. So they successfully repurchased the land without paying over the odds and the place was soon producing copper. It's the kind of rags-to-riches story that we all dream of.'

But for most of those associated with the mine, the story was one of sheer hard work. At the start of each shift, the miners had to take a one- or two-hour journey down ladders and along low, dark passageways to get to their place of work. They extracted the ore by hand, using chisels, pickaxes, and sometimes gunpowder. Miners hacked or blasted out chunks of ore-bearing rock and loaded it on to wagons that transported it to the area where another group of workers — mainly women and children — chipped away to separate the ore from the rock. Long hours and low pay were the norm, and in 1866 there was a strike over working conditions. There were few improvements and the strikers were forced to return to their jobs.

Most people have a mental image of the kind of architecture that was built in Cornwall to accommodate this sort of mining activity. Stark engine houses, their chimneys silhouetted against the sky, are pictured in countless books and travel brochures about the county. There are such sights at South Caradon, but there are also surprises. One such is Pearce's Engine House, which is propped with massive buttresses. The theory is that the engine's piston was angled so that each time it went down it pulled against the wall. So extra reinforcement was provided.

Jope's Engine House has strikingly ornate windows. They are a sign that the mine was prospering when the building was put up, and they encourage the visitor to look out for other places where the builders allowed themselves the luxury of elegance — for example in the masonry at the tops of some of the chimneys, good-quality work that has stood the test of time. The windows also remind one that the engine house manager would have wanted to look out of the building, to keep an eye on everything that was going on around him.

Another of these buildings, the Holman Engine House, owes its fame simply to the accidents of time. Removal and erosion of

Arched openings and rounded walls posed no problems for the skilled Cornish masons.

some of the masonry has produced an almost human shape, and those in the know look out for the silhouette of the 'Man in the Mine'. This is more than mere fancy. It is a reminder that for many, especially local people, places like South Caradon are full of memories of real people. The architecture is less important than the stories of those who worked there.

And, sometimes, who died there. Mining was a dangerous business and in the nineteenth century there was no requirement for a doctor to be on site or even nearby. The nearest doctor was based some thirty miles from South Caradon, and this could be too far to get the necessary help. For some, indeed, there could be little hope. In February 1862, Jane Husband went to work at the mine and entered the jigging house. Her dress was caught in the machinery and she was drawn in and crushed to death. The local paper reported that, remarkably, none of her bones seemed to be broken.

For others, better on-site treatment might have made all the difference. In 1870, worker John Oliver slipped and caught his foot in a flywheel that had just been fitted in one of the engine houses. As the wheel turned, it dragged him round, breaking both his legs in the process. As the local newspaper put it, 'He was placed under medical treatment, but he died almost as soon as he reached his own door. He leaves a wife and eight children.'

A restored mine would be a fitting memorial to such men and women. The plan is for long-term conservation – removing ivy and other plant growth from the buildings, stabilising structures, and repointing. A programme to make dangerous shafts safe and to develop proper footpaths around the site would be put into place. And information would be provided about the mine's history and significance.

Martin Eddy was quick to point out the potential benefits to the local community of restoring the mine. 'We have a very low average income in Cornwall and we very much hope that the mine will bring more money into the area. Our vision is that visitors will come to South Caradon, make for themselves the magical discovery of the mine in its man-made valley, and learn something about its history. And put some money into the local economy in the process.'

The most dramatic silhouettes occur where openings have been enlarged to remove machinery from the engine houses.

At Poltimore House, the south-western building that reached the *Restoration* final last year, there was great public interest after the building was featured in the first series. Amongst the visitors who came to the house were many who had been pupils when Poltimore was a girls' school and a number who had been born there when it was a maternity hospital, confirming the interest in the recent history of the house as well as its grand beginnings. Meanwhile, with the building still under threat, its custodians have applied for a grant to provide a temporary roof covering to protect the structure from the elements. At the same time, discussions have continued about a viable use for Poltimore. One possible solution is to convert the upper floors to apartments to generate income while setting up a training centre for heritage interpreters – such as guides and living-history practitioners – downstairs.

At Arnos Vale Cemetery in Bristol, a great deal of work has been done by volunteers. Large areas have been cleared up and dangerous parts of the cemetery have been fenced off to protect visitors. Bristol City Council, which acquired the site by compulsory purchase, is in talks with the previous owner about obtaining the cemetery records and Books of Remembrance. In addition, surveyors are in the process of looking at the various buildings on the site, to assess the work that needs doing.

The Building Preservation Trust for the Whitfield Tabernacle, the eighteenth-century chapel that is so important in the history of religious nonconformity, has spent the recent months revising its plans in order to resubmit a bid to the Heritage Lottery Fund. It has appointed a project officer to work alongside the architect and draw up the various strategy documents – from conservation plan to business plan – that are required. The Trust has focused on a future for the Tabernacle that combines community use for the main space, which could be hired by all sorts of local groups, with an interpretation centre where schools, students, and others could come to learn about the history of nonconformist religion.

RESTORATION

T^{HE} SOUTH EAST

Archbishop's Palace CHARING

Strawberry Hill TWICKENHAM

Severndroog Castle SHOOTER'S HILL

In the South East it is hard to get away from the feeling that you are at one of Britain's centres of power. In terms of money and influence, it is the richest of the British regions. It is uniquely dominated by London, the capital city to which all roads and railway lines seem to lead, which is still the seat of political power, the country's biggest employer, and a trendsetter in matters ranging from design to politics.

The South East also includes Canterbury, the headquarters of the English Church, and in earlier centuries this made the region perhaps even more important. In the Middle Ages, monarch and archbishop were the two most powerful people in the kingdom. And in times when travel was difficult and slow, the South East benefited from being close to continental Europe, on direct lines of communication with France and more distant powers such as the Pope in Rome.

The restoration candidates from the South East reflect this focus on centres of power. Two of the three are in London and the other owes its existence to the archbishops of Canterbury. They all, in their different ways, represent the far-reaching influence of this most dynamic of British regions.

The most ancient is the Archbishop's Palace at Charing in Kent. When it was built in the Middle Ages it was just one of the residences of the head of the English Church, but a

All the elements of the eighteenth-century Gothic Revival are present at Strawberry Hill – an irregular plan, pointed window openings, towers, turrets, and battlements.

The building at the end of the driveway (opposite, top) is the old Archbishop's Palace, now surrounded by a cluster of medieval and later buildings in Charing, Kent.

particularly important one because it stood on the route between the two cities of London and Canterbury. So the archbishop used the house frequently when journeying from one city to the other and the place regularly played host to prominent guests including kings, high churchmen, and diplomats.

The other two restoration candidates in this region, although both in London today were originally just outside the capital, which has grown to envelop them. Strawberry Hill, the house of writer, collector, and tastemaker Horace Walpole, is in Twickenham. In the mid-eighteenth century, when Walpole started his years of building work on the house, Twickenham was a centre of taste. Walpole gathered a circle of influential artists and designers around him. The poet Alexander Pope lived nearby. The artistic influence of these men was extraordinary – their work became known all over the country and beyond, changing taste in all sorts of ways. In particular Walpole's house, the focus and inspiration of this movement, started a fashion for Gothic architecture in a new guise. Strawberry Hill is one of the most influential buildings in the history of English architecture and design.

Severndroog Castle on Shooter's Hill in south-east London is a much more modest building, a folly in the grounds of a vanished country estate. To the casual observer, this eighteenth-century Gothic tower looks more like a frivolity than a symbol of power or influence. And yet it was built by a widow as a memorial to her husband and his achievements with the East India Company, the organisation that laid the foundations of the British Empire. Sir William James, whose widow built Severndroog, defeated pirates on the western coast of India, making the area safe for shipping where others had failed. Far from frivolous, his success was a matter of life and death for those who sailed off Mumbai and Goa.

So the three South Eastern restoration candidates symbolise in very different ways the influence of the region – one deriving from the power of the Church, one the power of the Empire, and one the importance of culture. All were associated with people who spread their influence far and wide. Today they deserve equally widespread support.

The Gothic Revival style seen at Strawberry Hill also shaped Severndroog Castle, shrouded by trees on a south London hilltop.

Archbishop's Palace

In the Middle Ages the Archbishop of Canterbury was the richest and most powerful man in England after the king. The archbishops held around one hundred and fifty manors, commanding a huge income from farming. They could draw on the wealth of the Church, which took one tenth of the income of everyone in the country, in cash or kind. They were also powerful statesmen, usually highly intelligent men, whose influence was felt throughout England and beyond. It is not surprising that some of these church leaders found little time for spiritual matters.

The medieval archbishops spent most of their time either at Canterbury or at their palace and church at Lambeth, across the river from London. But they had many other properties, and one of the most important was at Charing, a comfortable day's ride outside Canterbury on the road to London.

One of the main uses for palaces like that at Charing was entertaining. As head of the Church in England, the archbishop had regular meetings with other churchmen – both English abbots and bishops and clergymen from abroad. He also had to entertain guests from the secular world, including the king himself. And if the court came to stay, the archbishop had to have enough accommodation to put up dozens of servants. But most of all, he needed a great hall in which to hold big meetings and banquets.

The Church held land at Charing at least as early as the eighth century. The first house here was probably built by Lanfranc, the man who came from Normandy to be archbishop in the time of William the Conqueror. But the earliest fragments of stonework on the site today date from the twelfth or thirteenth centuries. These fragments, a wall and window arch and part of what was the archbishop's private chapel, are precious. Very little domestic architecture has survived from this period and what has survived is usually either in poor condition or has been so thoroughly restored as to have little of its original character. The early remains at Charing are in remarkably good condition.

But the heyday of the palace came rather later, in the fourteenth and early fifteenth centuries. By this time, the archbishops were often men who put the affairs of state

From this angle (above) the complex looks utilitarian. There seems little evidence of medieval grandeur and every sign that these are farm buildings, pure and simple.

But here (left) the hall's past is clear to see. The frame and tracery of a magnificent medieval window, later blocked and re-pierced with a smaller opening, is preserved.

Inside the hall, the roof is a forest of ancient oak braces and rafters. Their strong timber, firmly pegged together, has survived the centuries remarkably well.

before spiritual matters. They were diplomats and bureaucrats who wrestled with the running of a large church organisation, with the Church's relations with the state, and with the relationship between the English Church and the Pope in Rome. They were usually highly educated men, often hand-picked for high office in the Church. More and more, they needed an appropriate setting in which to operate.

And so, in the late thirteenth century, the palace at Charing was rebuilt in a manner fitting to the status of its occupant. The archbishop of the time, Robert Winchelsea, used the latest style of architecture. It was Gothic, the style of pointed arches that had been used for over a century, but the latest version of Gothic, the highly ornate mode now known as the Decorated style. Winchelsea's masons used it to create one of the most magnificent houses in the kingdom.

At the heart of the palace was the largest room, the great hall. In an early medieval home the hall *was* the house. It was a large room where everyone ate and slept and where the lord or archbishop transacted his business. But by Winchelsea's time, great lords had begun to build themselves private living apartments and dormitory accommodation for their servants. The hall was used mainly for grand occasions such as banquets. For a powerful lord or church leader, it was important to have a magnificent hall in which such events could be properly staged.

Although it has been used for three hundred years as a barn, there are still hints in the hall at Charing of its original magnifi-cence. Most of the guests would have entered through the two-storeyed porch. The dressed-stone details stand out from the main walls, which are made of flint. This might well have been rendered originally, although some of the surfaces are so smooth and well finished that they may have formed the finished surface. Either way, they indicate a building that has been well constructed.

In the hall itself, the one remaining medieval window is tall and its tracery would have been beautifully carved. Instead of the double-pitched roof of today, supported by a row of wooden posts, there would have been a magnificent single-span timber roof. Some of the corbels, the protruding stones that supported the timbers, can still be seen – some carved with leaf forms, others with oxen or human heads – although most are very worn.

It is not too hard to imagine this great room as it was in the time of Robert Winchelsea. The flint walls would have been covered with lime plaster and this might have been decorated with murals or covered with hangings. There would have been heat – and plenty of smoke – from a central fire, and the floor would have been covered with straw mixed with rue (as a disinfectant) and lavender (for its perfume). The archbishop and his guests would have sat at the top table, set at one end like the high table at an Oxbridge college. More lowly members of the households of both the archbishop and his guests would take their places at the other tables running the length of the great room. And very impressed they would have been, because at 21 metres in length the hall was second only to the one belonging to the king, Westminster Hall at the heart of the Palace of Westminster and now part of the Houses of Parliament.

The hall was only part of a complex of buildings which still survive on the site, as part of the farmhouse, as ancillary farm buildings, or as ruins. The buildings surround an irregularly shaped courtyard entered through a gatehouse with a large arch for carts and carriages, a smaller one for people on foot. The entrance way would have been vaulted in stone – the remains of one rib can be seen in a corner. Above, on what was the first floor, was a room with a fireplace, quite a luxury for the porter's accommodation.

Beyond the main group of buildings, the site's old perimeter wall, made of similar rubble masonry to that seen in the hall, still survives in part.

Repeated alterations and changes of use have led to many extensions and changes – and many of these can be seen in the walls. Several medieval windows have been blocked, some with stone infill, others, blocked later, with brick. This material was also used for extensions and repairs to the walls. But amidst all this many ancient details, like the charming medieval quatrefoil opening, still survive.

The buildings around the courtyard are mostly in ruins, but there are several interesting features. The west range, for example, contains the remains of lodgings and garderobes, the medieval lavatories that must have drained away into the nearby stream, presumably via a lost system of conduits so that the waste material was kept away from the fresh-water supply. Elsewhere, behind the farmhouse, remains of the archbishop's chapel survive, its undercroft used as a farm shed.

These ruins tell the story of the decline of the palace at Charing. During the Middle Ages it was an important place. Henry VII visited it regularly, and the archbishop of the time, John Morton, extended and improved the buildings. Charing was also visited by Henry VIII, most notably in 1513, when he was on his way to the Field of the Cloth of Gold in northern France, a meeting and festival held by the kings of France, Spain, and England. Later Henry took over the property for his personal use and it remained in Crown hands until the seventeenth century, after which it was sold and turned into a farm.

A building as old as the Archbishop's Palace deserves to be maintained with special care. Because it has been used as a farm for several hundred years there have been few major

alterations. When restoration takes place there will not be the common problem about what to do with Victorian additions that get in the way of the earlier remains but also have historical interest of their own.

But restoration will still be a challenge. There are major cracks in two corners of the great hall, cracks that may have begun in the Middle Ages as a result of the strain caused by the large roof. Thanks to an emergency grant from English Heritage, temporary scaffolding is keeping the wall upright, but a more permanent solution will be needed soon.

Once the structural problems have been solved, the building can be put to good use for the local community. The Parish Council can use one of the buildings. The great hall can become a community venue, generating income through being hired for special events. Farmers' markets could take place on the green in front of the complex. In the centre of a beautiful old village, near a medieval church and surrounded by old houses, the old palace is at the heart of one of the most beautiful small towns in the South East. If restoration can go ahead it will also be able to take its place at the heart of the local community once more.

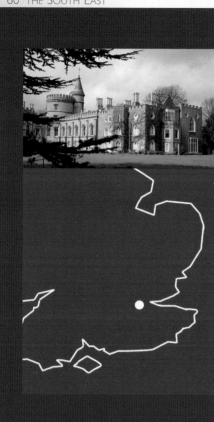

Strawberry Hill

Horace Walpole was young, brilliant, and very well connected. His father, Sir Robert Walpole, was Britain's first Prime Minister. Horace was educated at Eton and King's College, Cambridge. He went on the grand tour with the poet Thomas Gray, a friend from Eton. He was a Member of Parliament. But he was above all devoted to the arts and literature and when he was 30, in 1747, he moved to Twickenham, where Strawberry Hill, an extravagant fantasy of a house that came to inspire and symbolise an entire movement in British taste — a movement originating in the Gothic style of the Middle Ages.

Many designers and patrons in the mid-eighteenth century were fascinated by the Gothic style. Instead of the straight classical lines, pediments, and moulded cornices of the typical Georgian house, they were interested in pointed arches, turrets, pinnacles, and vaults. But they did not copy slavishly the Gothic of the medieval cathedrals. They took details from many different medieval buildings, modified them, and combined them with Georgian features. A window copied from a design in Salisbury Cathedral might be given wooden shutters, to combine Gothic elegance with Georgian comfort. A vault might get a new pattern of ribs. Or a fireplace from a medieval great hall could be reduced in scale to fit into a Georgian room.

So eighteenth-century Gothic is a theatrical, stage-set idea of Gothic, in which details formerly in stone could be carved in wood or moulded in papier mâché. The possibilities were endless, and this is what appealed to Walpole. He embarked on a study of Gothic buildings, both at first hand and from illustrations. And he began to make his plans.

Walpole worked in an unusual way. He neither employed a single architect to design his house nor did he design it himself. Instead Walpole gathered around him a group of like-minded friends, a 'Committee of Taste', on whose advice he drew. The principal member of the group was John Chute, who, like Walpole, was a gentleman, a connoisseur, and a designer. Together, Walpole and Chute conceived a dramatic exterior to transform the existing house into a Gothic fantasy. Battlements and wooden pinnacles dominated the skyline. Ornate Gothic windows pierced the walls. This first phase took until 1753 and

The long gallery is sumptuous, with its traceried canopies based on a medieval tomb in Canterbury Cathedral, its floor with inlays of brass, and its rich ceiling copied from Henry VII's chapel in Westminster Abbey. But the rich wallcoverings are in need of repair.

gave Walpole the core of his house. Two further building phases followed in Walpole's lifetime, the first from 1758 to 1766 and the second from 1772 to 1776.

Inside the opulence was – and is – staggering. One set-piece room after another takes the breath away. From the first phase, Walpole's own favourite was the staircase. This was originally

Details show the exterior of the Long Gallery and Round Tower, an ornate window from Walpole's earliest alterations to the house, and one of Walpole's heraldic beasts.

decorated in a plain stone colour, with Gothic tracery (derived from Prince Arthur's tomb in Worcester Cathedral) painted in repeating patterns up the walls. The balustrade, though, contains tracery from a totally different, continental source. Such a mixture of sources was typical of Walpole, and shows how his principal interest was to create a fantastic, intoxicating effect, not a sober imitation of an earlier style.

Another important room for Walpole was the library, its bookcases topped with pinnacles like medieval tombs. Walpole owned thousands of books and it was important to him that they were nobly shelved and properly arranged. This room also shows another of his passions – history. The library ceiling is emblazoned with coats of arms, some belonging to his real ancestors, others fictional creations, belonging to the mythical 'Counts of Strawberry Hill', about whom Walpole liked to fantasise.

The magnificent interiors of the 1760s phase include the long gallery, a rich composition of red wallcoverings topped with gilded fan vaulting. Although this decorative scheme is just as extravagant as the earlier ones, it is different in one respect, because here Walpole drew his main inspiration from a single extant medieval building – Henry VII's chapel at Westminster Abbey. This building formed the model for many of the details in the room, notably the fan vaults on the room's ceiling, encrusted with tracery, which are directly modelled on those in the chapel.

Some scholars have seen the influence of two of Walpole's friends on these interiors. In the earlier rooms they detect the fanciful sensibility of Richard Bentley, who also designed Gothic furniture for Strawberry Hill. Their ornate decoration, full of flamboyant crocketed pinnacles, seems typical of Bentley. In the later rooms, however, John Chute appears to have been the main influence. But even Chute's more 'correct' interiors are elaborate and over the top. So the impression given by Walpole's work as a whole is of a fantastical stage set. Even apparently practical items such as fireplaces were sometimes made purely for show. Several fireplaces at Strawberry Hill, based on engravings of real medieval ones, are carved in wood rather than stone. No fires could have burned in their grates and Walpole recalled in his letters that guests often felt the cold.

Today, in need of restoration, the house is delightful to visit. To contemporaries, the visual effect must have been staggering. Visitors entered the house through rooms painted to resemble stone. The lighting was kept low and the stained glass created a warm atmosphere, producing an effect that Walpole liked to describe as 'gloomth', a combination of gloom and warmth. To pass from these rooms to chambers such as the long gallery, with their lavish, colour-themed decoration, would have been to experience something unlike any other interior. Strawberry Hill was soon the talk of the town. Walpole had friends everywhere and was a brilliant and prolific letter-writer. He lived in a fashionable district that, thanks to the presence of luminaries such as the poet Alexander Pope, was becoming a centre of taste. Walpole's fictional writings, notably the Gothic novel *The Castle of Otranto*, spread the fashion for the Gothic still further.

The bookcases in the library, with their filigree tracery, were based on an engraving in a book about Old St Paul's Cathedral.

So news of Walpole's achievement travelled fast. Soon, Walpole had illustrations made of his rooms, commissioning the watercolour artist John Carter to make a full record of the decoration of the house. This was the first such complete record, one that has become an invaluable source for historians as well as an inspiration for later artists and home-owners. As Anna Chalcraft explained, 'The fact that Walpole's inventory has been kept, together with paintings and drawings, and that records were regularly updated, provides a unique archive covering the history of the house, its decoration, and its contents. As conservators and restorers examine the fabric, they will be able to check with the records to find the precise date of each change of decoration, the person who did the work, and even how much it cost.'

Before long, designs based on details of Strawberry Hill were appearing in pattern books, on which other designers drew for inspiration or imitation. Many was the gentleman who wanted a window, a chimney piece, or a garden building done in the style made fashionable by Walpole. 'Strawberry Hill Gothic' was all the rage.

Walpole led fashion in other ways. When wooden panelling was the most common wallcovering, he was an enthusiast for wallpaper. Rather than use the simple small repeating patterns that were current in eighteenth-century wallpaper, Walpole went for more lavish effects – rococo designs influenced by Venetian damasks and, of course, Gothic motifs. His accounts of the 1750s show that he bought wallpaper from Thomas Bromwich, a leading manufacturer based in London. Rarely before had Bromwich's products been used in such luxurious surroundings.

Another material that Walpole made fashionable was papier mâché. In medieval Gothic buildings, vaults were usually made of stone, but a stone vault was very heavy, needing a system of buttresses for support. Papier mâché allowed Walpole to reproduce all the crisp details of stone vaulting in a lightweight material. Again, Walpole drew on the services of Thomas Bromwich, whose firm also produced papier mâché, supplying ready-made ornaments to builders. At Strawberry Hill, however, Bromwich worked to the designs of Walpole and Chute, spending four years making the ceiling of the long gallery.

In the Round Tower (opposite), panelling, window reveals, doorcases, and doors are all covered with Gothic detailing.

The door and windows in the Little Parlour (above) display the double curve or ogee shape, drawn from Gothic buildings of the fourteenth century.

The staircase ceiling (below) is studded with fleurs-de-lys.

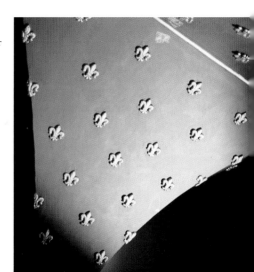

A fantasia of arches, gilded crockets, and tracery covers the doorway and fireplace in Walpole's bedchamber.

Fashionable materials such as papier mâché and wallpaper were combined at Strawberry Hill with traditional ones, such as stained glass. Walpole was a keen collector of stained glass and examples of English, Dutch, and Flemish glass, some dating from the sixteenth century, were installed in the windows, flooding coloured light into the interiors. Again, other connoisseurs caught Walpole's enthusiasm and amongst the men of taste who incorporated old glass into their homes were Sir John Soane at his house in Lincoln's Inn Fields and Sir Walter Scott at Abbotsford.

By 1792 Walpole had doubled the size of his house. A compulsive collector, he filled it with his possessions, which ranged from his library to collections of prints, and all sorts of items of historical interest. When his collection was finally sold in 1842, the sale lasted thirty-two days. It seemed that the heyday of both house and collection was finally over.

But the house was to have a new lease of life as the home of Lady Waldegrave, an enthusiast for Gothic who set about restoring the house in the mid-nineteenth century, redecorating the library and gallery and building a new wing to accommodate her guests. By this time, architects were designing in a much more 'correct' form of Gothic than Walpole's. But Lady Waldegrave preferred the work of the Committee of Taste, and her rooms are just as fanciful in their way as Walpole's originals. Lady Waldegrave even bought back some of the original owner's collection, and the expanded Strawberry Hill proved an ideal venue for her entertaining. But after her death in 1879 the house suffered from neglect until, in 1923, it became a Roman Catholic teacher-training college. It still accommodates St Mary's College, now part of the University of Surrey.

Strawberry Hill had a huge influence. It was the first house designed completely in the Gothic style, both inside and out, the first to have a deliberately asymmetrical plan, the first to have a guidebook. Its owners, including St Mary's College, have looked after its structure, but its interiors are now in a perilous state. Like any building of its age, it will suffer if it is left for long unmaintained. And some of its interiors have not been touched since the nineteenth century. The vision of those who care for Strawberry Hill is to preserve the house and open it to the public.

A detail of one of the windows shows how ancient glass was reused. Some of the pieces were complete panels, many painted with coats of arms, animals, or fruit. Others were tiny fragments arranged for decorative effect.

Michael Snodin, architectural historian and chairman of the Friends of Strawberry Hill.

The Strawberry Hill Trust was formed initially to commission a feasibility study, and this study came to the conclusion that a Building Preservation Trust would be the best type of body to save and open the house. The Strawberry Hill Trust is therefore in discussion with St Mary's College about the possibility of taking out a lease on the house. As well as conserving the house and opening it to the public, the Trust is also keen for the educational potential of the house to be realised, and for the building to be used for all levels of education. There are already strong links with Yale University, which holds the world's most important collection of Walpole's books, manuscripts, and possessions. At last, the prospects seem good for the house to receive the care and conservation it so obviously deserves.

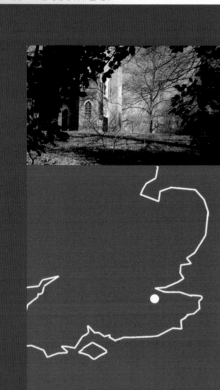

Severndroog Castle

It is like a fish out of water, an eighteenth-century Gothic tower atop Shooter's Hill amongst the suburbs of south-east London. Thousands pass it every day, but few stop to learn why it was built or why it has such a bizarre name. To them it is simply a folly – a building that expresses the eccentricity of some rich family from the past.

But it is a building with huge possibilities. Dr Barry Gray, chairman of the Building Preservation Trust working to save the

castle, explained: 'It has huge potential – a fairy-tale Gothic castle in the middle of London. The site is also fascinating: it is set amidst ancient woodland and there have probably been trees here since the end of the last Ice Age. Visitors to the castle would be able to study these trees at every level, from ground to canopy.'

Like most follies, Severndroog Castle is a building with a very specific purpose, but one that is not obvious to the casual observer. One of the fascinating things about the building is that its inspiration is as interesting as its architecture. It is also special because of its site. Over the centuries many follies were built in London. But pressures of space and repeated new developments have meant that most of them have disappeared. Severndroog remains, and is one of the earliest follies in the capital.

So how did it come to be built? Severndroog Castle owes its existence to the career of Sir William James, seaman, commodore of the Bombay Marine in the British East India Company, and scourge of pirates on the high seas. Little doubt is left by the inscription on the stone tablet above the door:

This building was Erected MDCCLXXXIV by the
Representative
of the late
WILLIAM JAMES Bart.
To commemorate that Gallant Officer's
atchievements in the
EAST INDIES
during his command of the Company's Marine
Forces in those Seas
And in a particular manner to Record the
Conquest of
The CASTLE OF SEVERNDROOG off the COAST of
MALABAR
which fell to his Superior Valour and able
Conduct
on the 2nd Day of April MDCCLV

So this remarkable building is a memorial to a remarkable career. William James was the son of a miller, who grew up in rural Wales and dreamed of going to sea. At the age of 12 he

Viewed from the corner (opposite), the tower's unusual shape is clear. It is built on a triangular plan, with hexagonal turrets at each corner.

The tower overlooks the branches of ancient trees, making it an ideal observation platform for the ecologist.

fulfilled his dream, starting as a deckhand. Six years later he was serving in the West Indies under William Hawke, who gave him his first command.

But it was in the East Indies that James was to become famous. By 1751 he was commander-in-chief of the Bombay Marine, which was effectively the private army of the East India Company, the organisation through which Britain both traded and acquired territory in India. For centuries there had been a problem with piracy off the west coast of India, between Mumbai and Goa. In the early eighteenth century these seas were dominated by the Angria family, African Muslim pirates who were making a fortune from robbing passing British ships and extorting protection money. They were based on the island of Vijayadrug, also known as Savardrug (or Severndroog), south of Mumbai.

Some of the windows are false (above) and exist just to balance the tower's façades. But all the details, from the hood mould at the top to the sill at the bottom, were carefully reproduced.

A plain, but unmistakably Gothic, window throws light on to the turret stairs (right).

Bird droppings are a problem here, as in so many abandoned buildings.

When he first encountered the pirates, James, unlike so many before him, refused to be cowed. With a formidable show of strength he gave chase, forced them to retreat to their fortress, and resolved to return and defeat them in battle. So in late March 1755 James headed for Savardrug, bombarded the fort and captured the island on 2 April. In the following months the Bombay Marine and Royal Navy joined forces and destroyed most of the other pirate forts in the area. Eight years later James retired to Eltham, dying suddenly of a stroke in 1778.

James's widow – the 'Representative' mentioned in the inscription – decided to build a tower to commemorate her husband. As architect she chose Richard Jupp. He was not an especially well-known architect, but had designed parts of Guy's Hospital and had worked on the house at Painshill Park in Surrey, a building in grounds that are studded with follies. In addition, since 1768 he had been surveyor to the East India Company and this must have made him an obvious choice.

The tops of the turrets are adorned with another Gothic detail, tiny quatrefoil windows.

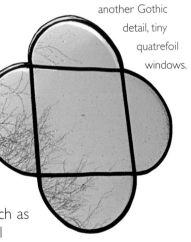

Jupp created a striking building for Lady James. From a distance it looks like a square structure, but in fact it is a three-sided brick tower with hexagonal turrets at each of its corners. Its battlements make it look like a castle and its pointed windows are in the Gothic taste. But these are generously wide eighteenth-century Gothic windows, not the slender lancets or arrow-slits of a medieval castle – there were good views to be had from the site on Shooter's Hill, and Jupp wanted to make the most of them. Other charming details, such as the fanlight with its lattice of glazing bars and the small quatrefoil windows beneath the battlements, mark the building as a classic piece of eighteenth-century Gothic.

The building has three floors, reached via a spiral staircase in one of the corner towers, plus a viewing platform on the roof. This vantage point is 63 feet above the ground and the hilltop site means that the top is actually rather higher above sea level than the top of the dome of St Paul's. This makes the views from the tower outstanding, encompassing parts of Kent, Surrey, and Essex, as well as the capital itself.

The boarding on the roof is loose and unsafe – full repairs will be needed before visitors can admire the view.

To keep out the damp both leading and downpipes will need to be overhauled.

Inside, Lady James created a fitting memorial to her late husband. The ground floor contained a small museum, with displays including arms, armour, and other artefacts from the battle at Savardrug. The first floor had a painted ceiling, which told the story of the battle in six separate sections. The upper floor was furnished in what was described in the eighteenth century as the 'modern taste', and it must have formed a comfortable viewing gallery for those who did not want to risk the wind and rain on the roof. The whole ensemble, Gothic tower and memorial collection, was very much of its time, an admirable window on the world of Sir William and a worthy memorial to an eighteenth-century hero.

Sir William's widow had the tower built so that she could see it from the family house in the valley below. As well as a memorial it was also a summerhouse. The James's house has long since disappeared – a railway station now stands on its site. But Severndroog Castle remains, a reminder of the great man for those who will stop and read the inscription above the door.

In its exposed position on Shooter's Hill it is also a building that was, and remains, easy for the public to see and admire. This makes it rather unusual, since the traditional location for a folly is at the heart of a country estate, where it can be seen from the big house and glimpsed on a hilltop by people on public roads far away. Getting close to a folly is often difficult.

At Severndroog, public access has a long history. In 1816 the castle was sold to John Blades, a local man who gave the public free access to the grounds, and this continued until about 1850. The building came into public ownership in 1922 when it was bought by the London County Council and opened as a tea room and observation tower. Its usefulness was recognised during both World Wars, when it was used for observation – during World War II it housed radar equipment.

Over the last twenty years the building has suffered from neglect. Thieves have removed the lead guttering, making rainwater pour down the walls and causing damage to the brickwork. Water penetration has also meant that the floors and ceilings are rotting away, and birds have got in leaving mess to join the damage caused by human vandals. During the time of the Greater London Council some restoration work was

Although much work is needed inside, details such as doors and architraves remain.

carried out on the middle floor, preserving ornate plasterwork and finely painted details, but the problems with the rest of the structure put this as much at risk as the rest of the building. Clearly, with the tower in such a state, public access is impossible for health and safety reasons and the building stands closed and apparently unloved.

Dr Barry Gray on one of the castle's hexagonal turrets.

But there are plenty of people who do love Severndroog Castle and the Building Preservation Trust is campaigning to save the building. When the local council wanted to lease the building to a private developer who planned to convert the tower to offices, a petition was started and, in two weeks, some five thousand signatures were collected. Funding has been raised to do a survey and compile a feasibility study, the first step towards restoring the building. Barry Gray explained that plans include restoration, the provision of new café facilities, and making the building accessible to the disabled. It is hoped to make the castle sustainable from the income from the café, plus fees for hiring the building for events such as weddings. 'Above all,' said Dr Gray, 'we want to guarantee public access.' There is much to do, but Severndroog Castle is not a huge building and its many supporters are confident that it can be restored. They will be doing a great service to London if they achieve their aim.

RESTORATION Update South East
News from the first series

Wilton's, the Victorian music hall in Whitechapel that reached the final of the last series, reported a very good public response after the building was featured on *Restoration*. There was tremendous support locally, with a number of small donations and offers of help. In addition many people – often locals – who did not know that Wilton's existed have been shown around the building and experienced its magic at first hand. But there are relatively few chances to see performances at Wilton's, although there have been some as part of the Spitalfields Festival. The building is too fragile, and too reliant on 'temporary' repairs done in 1999, to take very much use. So the need for restoration is urgent and funding is now being sought from the Heritage Lottery Fund.

The Darnley Mausoleum in Kent was in a way one of the more problematic restoration candidates in the first series of *Restoration*. A perfect eighteenth-century mausoleum designed by the architect James Wyatt, it was intended to hold the remains of a British aristocrat and his family. It was never used for this intended purpose, but neither was it suitable for any other use, remaining isolated and increasingly unloved, the target of vandals and arsonists. Unlike many buildings, it does not lend itself to conversion to a new use that could generate income. But it cries out to be restored so that visitors can appreciate its beauty once more. It is therefore pleasing to report that the building, and the historic Cobham Park in which it stands, together with other historic buildings in the park, are to receive a grant of £5 million from the Heritage Lottery Fund. This represents 75 per cent of the cost of restoring the mausoleum and historic park and providing facilities such as a visitor shelter, warden's accommodation, and car parking. The future of this extraordinary building is assured.

In Enfield, north London, the local council have given planning consent for the proposed restoration scheme at Broomfield House, where the project includes a community education centre, café, and function room. The work of putting together bids for major funding is now under way, with a substantial contribution of £1 million to come from the council itself. The local supporters of the house have also been creating a higher media profile for the building, and two prominent figures, physician and broadcaster Lord Winston and film-maker David Puttnam, have become patrons of the project. With such high-level support, locals are hopeful that this still very fragile building will once more become a worthy centre of its park and a community facility of which everyone can be proud.

RESTORATION

The Midlands and East Anglia

Newstead Abbey NEWSTEAD

Old Grammar School
and Saracen's Head KING'S NORTON

Bawdsey Radar Station BAWDSEY

This region takes in a vast swathe of central England, from the Welsh Marches to the coast of Suffolk. It is impossible to generalise about such a broad area, which encompasses the industrial heartlands of the Midlands and the rich agricultural land of East Anglia, and which includes within its architectural heritage the timber-framed cottages and stone border castles of the West, the factories of Birmingham, and the vast medieval churches of Norfolk and Suffolk.

But one can say at least that this region has been, culturally as geographically, at the heart of England for hundreds of years. In the Middle Ages, cathedral cities such as Norwich and Lichfield were centres of both spirituality and power, while prosperous towns such as Coventry were focal points for trade. In the eighteenth and nineteenth centuries the Midlands became the country's industrial heart, as mining and manufacturing flourished in areas such as Shropshire, where the latest metalworking technology made possible the construction of the world's first iron bridge. Meanwhile, the most up-to-date agricultural techniques were being applied in East Anglia to make farming more efficient and to help feed the country's growing population. In both town and country, these heartland regions were at the cutting edge.

Many a country house was built on the site of a former abbey, but at few is this more obvious than at Newstead, where the west front of the church adjoins the entrance front of the house.

Today, with much of the manufacturing industry gone and farming in crisis, the region needs the ability to innovate more than ever. It is certainly acquiring innovative buildings, like Birmingham's recent Selfridge's store, with its curving, shimmering façade designed by Future Systems. But it is also looking after its heritage. Birmingham's Jewellery Quarter contains some excellent examples of old industrial buildings saved by being put to new uses. This chapter highlights three further potential restoration projects.

The first candidate is a building that is most famous for its links with a famous poet – Lord Byron's Newstead Abbey. This building has already undergone a radical change of use, having been turned into a country house, like so many other monastic buildings, after the dissolution of the monasteries in the sixteenth century. So next to the ancient abbey church is a notable house, converted from the abbey outbuildings in Tudor times and added to over the following three centuries. The part of the structure most immediately at risk is the façade of the abbey church, a beautiful example of Early English Gothic architecture that is simply crumbling away. Its combination of elegant proportions and high-quality stone carving makes it unique. But pollution is attacking its stones and it needs urgent attention if future generations are to enjoy the view that inspired the building's one-time owner.

Next come a pair of buildings in a suburb of Birmingham. The Old Grammar School at King's Norton and the neighbouring Saracen's Head are outstanding examples of the kind of timber-framed construction that was once very common in the West Midlands, an area where good building stone is scarce. Shropshire, Herefordshire, and Warwickshire still have towns and villages with entire streets of 'black-and-white' wood-framed houses, but it is a surprise to find them in a suburb of Birmingham. They have much to tell us about the architecture and construction of late-medieval buildings. But they also played an important role in the history of the area. They had a particular heyday in the seventeenth century, when the area was run by an influential Puritan teacher who made King's Norton, for a while, a notable centre of learning — one more reason for saving these precious, beautiful, and fragile buildings.

For the region's final building we jump forward to the twentieth century, to the years leading up to World War II. The radar station at Bawdsey on the Suffolk coast was the first in the world and one of the sites where radar was developed. Work was already well under way when the public was made aware in no uncertain terms of the necessity of detecting enemy bombers. During the Spanish Civil War the bombardment of the northern Spanish town of Guernica in April 1937 shocked the world, but by this time secret research at Bawdsey was already well advanced. The buildings at the Bawdsey centre are modest, mostly low concrete and brick huts and underground structures. But they are important for what went on there, the creation of a technology that transformed warfare and saved millions of lives.

The buildings at King's Norton are striking examples of medieval timber framing — quite unexpected on the edge of Birmingham.

Radar pioneers at Bawdsey made the skies safer for British aircraft during World War II, and an early RAF sign remains as a reminder.

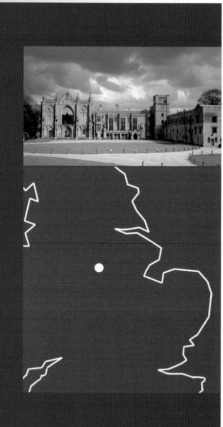

Newstead Abbey

It is a very unusual combination – the ruins of a medieval abbey with a country house, built in the sixteenth century and modified over succeeding centuries, attached to one side. The monastic remains include some of the most beautiful Gothic details in the Midlands. The house owes its fame to its links with one of the most famous of English writers, the poet Lord Byron. As Gillian Crawley, the general manager at Newstead, explained, no one knows why the builders of the house kept the abbey façade. It is one of the mysteries of the place, but a mystery that makes it one of the Midlands' most compelling buildings.

The story of Newstead Abbey spans more than eight hundred years. It was founded between 1164 and 1174 by King Henry II for an order known as the Augustinian (or Austin) Canons. The leader of their community was known as the prior and Newstead should therefore strictly be called a priory rather than an abbey. The canons lived in a monastic community but were also ordained priests and they saw it as part of their calling to do pastoral work in the wider community. Because they saw more of the outside world than the monks or nuns of other orders, the canons could take part in activities, such as saying regular masses for the dead of the local community, that brought in an income. So the canons were said to be financially richer than other orders. Their training for the priesthood meant in addition that they were amongst the best educated of all medieval monks.

As in any monastic community, the original buildings at Newstead centred on the church. Adjoining this was the cloister, the rectangular courtyard that linked the priory's other main structures, such as the refectory where the canons ate their meals, the chapter house where they held regular business meetings, and the warming room, one of the few parts of the priory that had a fire. Most of the medieval remains at Newstead date from around 1250, when an extensive rebuilding campaign began. The chapter house, parlour, and a large undercroft all date from this time, as does the most striking part of the old priory buildings, the Gothic west front of the church.

It is not hard to see why later residents of Newstead were attached to this front. Even in its ruined state it is a beautifully proportioned piece of medieval masonry. The architectural

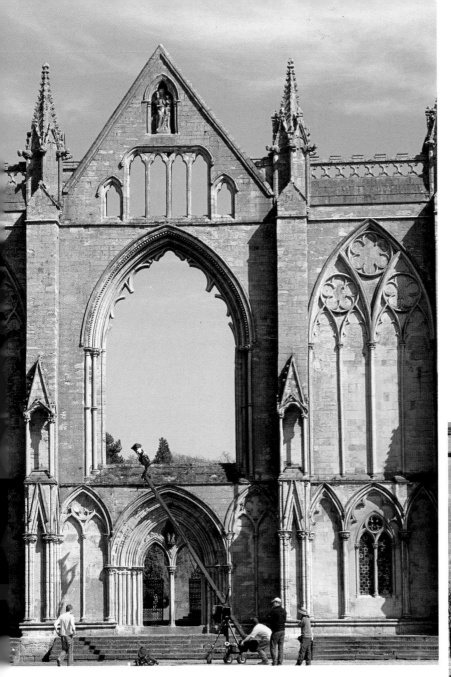

Against a backdrop of thirteenth-century arches and tracery, part of the *Restoration* team gets to work on filming the abbey façade.

In the cloister courtyard (below), Tudor and nineteenth-century work combine in harmony.

historian Nikolaus Pevsner called it 'an exceptionally perfect example of a late C13 church front'. Slender buttresses and elegant blank arcading on the ground floor lead the eye up to a vast central window. This opening lost its glass and its tracery centuries ago, but one can imagine what it looked like by glancing to either side. The central opening is flanked by a pair of beautifully designed blank windows. These were not designed to be glazed – their 'openings' are filled with stone, not glass, with the intention of creating a balanced effect on the front of the building. As a result they have survived intact,

and we can appreciate the pointed arches and geometrical patterns of their elaborate tracery, and imagine what the central glazed window would have looked like too. Still higher is the gable with its small statue of the Virgin Mary. Among the other surviving details are finely carved capitals, both in the stylised 'stiff-leaf' design of the early thirteenth century and in the more naturalistic manner of later in the century. This front must have been completed at the end of the thirteenth-century rebuilding, and the prior and canons must have been very pleased with the way in which it provided a fitting climax to the architecture of their church.

The west front was built in the manner of the time, and built to last. But the first threat to its survival came in 1539, when Henry VIII dissolved the English monasteries and presented Newstead to Sir John Byron of Colwick, a nobleman whom he praised for his 'good, true and faithful service'. Byron converted Newstead into a house, using the buildings around the cloister

The capitals carved with foliage, slender shafts, and deeply cut mouldings (opposite) add up to thirteenth-century work of the highest quality.

The impression in the cloister (below) is of a building that has grown over the centuries.

Light floods through one of the Tudor windows, forming shadows of mullions and glazing bars.

as the basis and stone from the church as raw material. As a result, many of the old monastic buildings were preserved as parts of Byron's house.

This was a rather unusual way to go about things. Many of Henry's courtiers simply used old monasteries as quarries, ransacking them for their stone and leaving the remains to fall down. Byron, for some reason, went about his conversion rather differently, and has left ample evidence of the priory's early history. He even left the beautiful west front standing – perhaps out of respect for the religious significance of the building – and it has been the most outstanding feature of the front of the house ever since.

Newstead passed through generations of the Byron family, with various Byrons adding and remodelling rooms. In the mid-eighteenth century the fifth Lord Byron, known as Mad Jack Byron, built a sham castle in the grounds and did much landscaping, but left the house in poor condition. On his death in 1798, the house, its buildings now in a ruinous state, was inherited by its most famous resident, the poet, the sixth Lord Byron.

Byron was only ten years old when he inherited Newstead. As a young man, and in spite of the success of his poetry, he had little money to restore the house and so limited himself to furnishing some of the smaller rooms. He was especially attached to his bedroom and dressing room, which adjoined the west front of the church and enabled him to hear the wind whistling through the great window at night. He hoped to acquire enough money to restore the house and, like Mad Jack Byron before him, got a servant to make excavations in the cloisters in the hope of finding buried gold, the fabled legacy of the wealthy Augustinians. But the only objects to be unearthed were human bones.

The poet was fond of Newstead, in spite of the fact that he used some of the rooms for target practice and reputedly let his animals – including a pet bear and his beloved dog, Boatswain – run wild through the house. He portrayed it as Norman Abbey in his masterpiece, the long, mock-epic poem *Don Juan*, and what comes out of his depiction is his love of the mixture of styles and rooms, the architectural hotch-potch, and the combination of irregularity and grandeur:

Huge halls, long galleries, spacious chambers, join'd
    By no quite lawful marriage of the Arts,
Might shock a Connoisseur; but when combined,
    Form'd a whole which, irregular in parts,
Yet left a grand impression on the mind,
    At least of those whose eyes are in their hearts . . .

Byron's rooms at the abbey were retained by Wildman and now have a late nineteenth-century atmosphere.

As his debts mounted, Byron realised that he would have to sell Newstead, and he found it hard to part with the place. But, in 1818, he sold the house to Thomas Wildman, who had come into a fortune from plantations that his family owned in Jamaica. At last Newstead was owned by someone with the money needed for its upkeep.

Wildman brought in a London architect, John Shaw, who restored the fabric and added extra rooms. In addition, Wildman and Shaw upgraded the front of the house, adding a further bay window and creating a more convenient ground-floor entrance to replace the previous one that gave access via

steps to the first floor. Otherwise, the Wildman family were restrained in their alterations – keen to respect Byron's legacy, they concentrated their efforts on the gardens. But the house only remained in the Wildman family until 1861, when it was sold by Wildman's widow. After several further changes of ownership, the building passed to the City of Nottingham. Gillian Crawley praised the way the local authority has looked after the property: 'The city fathers acted with foresight and generosity and the council has maintained Newstead, opening the house and grounds as a valued attraction close to the city.' And they kept the precious Byron collection: 'If the collections were to be broken up, it would be impossible to replace them.'

Newstead today is the legacy of the canons, the early Byrons who converted it to a house, the poet Byron, who left a unique collection of manuscripts and memorabilia, and Wildman, who cared for it and extended it. In its combination of medieval and nineteenth-century remains it is unique and its links with Byron, and the Byron collection housed there, give it an added importance. The whole house and the gardens and surrounding parkland need work, and various research projects are under way to establish what needs to be done. But it is clear that the most urgent need is for the repair of the precious west front of the medieval abbey. The Mansfield stone of which it is built, stone with a fine texture that makes it so

Rich carpets and curtains add warmth to the landing.

Byron family monuments from the sixteenth and seventeenth centuries, originally in nearby Colwick Church, are installed in the abbey's entrance hall.

good for carving, is also susceptible to pollution. Acid rain has attacked its surface, causing contour scaling, papery flakes of stone that detach themselves from the surface. In addition, iron clamps that hold some of the stonework together are corroding. The structure now poses a danger to visitors and has to be fenced off to protect them from falling stones.

The necessary conservation work is getting urgent. The more water that attacks the stone, the more unique medieval details will disappear for ever. And there is another problem. The Mansfield stone needed for the repairs is in short supply – it will need to be purchased soon, before the stocks are depleted much further. So quick action is needed, as Gillian Crawley put it, 'to give this icon back to the house and the landscape and to preserve this glorious building so that it can be enjoyed by future generations'. If these future visitors are to admire Newstead's architecture, to appreciate at first hand the grand impression that it made on Lord Byron, and to listen to the wind whistling through its windows, the abbey needs our care and support.

Old Grammar School and Saracen's Head

We tend to think of Birmingham as a city with a short history, famous for its expansion after the industrial revolution got under way. Its well-known buildings are mostly nineteenth-century or later, and there is nothing left of the ancient village green that occupied the site of the present Bull Ring. But go to the suburbs, the towns and villages that were absorbed as Birmingham spread, and it is a different story. King's Norton, about five miles to the south-west of the city centre, is a case in point. Although the area includes several large modern housing estates, at its heart lies a stunning group of three ancient buildings. The Church of St Nicholas has Norman origins and a beautiful fifteenth-century tower and spire. Next to it stand two buildings at risk, the former manor house now known as the Saracen's Head and the Old Grammar School. They are both remarkable structures that impress locals and visitors alike. Canon Rob Morris, rector of King's Norton, admiring the Old Grammar School referred to 'the quality of the timberwork, which has a strength and vitality about it unequalled in any building of similar size that I've seen'. Both these buildings have fascinating stories to tell.

It is likely that the Saracen's Head was the largest house in King's Norton in the fifteenth century. It was probably built by one of the area's richest cloth manufacturers and it is a superb example of a house belonging to a well-to-do late-medieval family. Later it became the manor house. King's Norton was a royal manor, so the house was home to the royal steward, the official who looked after the interests of the Crown. It was in this role that the house played host to Charles I's queen, Henrietta Maria, in 1629. Finally the house was sold, in the early nineteenth century, and part of it became an inn – hence its exotic name. Since 1930 it has been used by the church and local community as a meeting place and parish office.

So the Saracen's Head is a building that has grown and changed gradually over time and its fabric offers fascinating evidence of how this happened. The plan of the building is roughly in the shape of a capital H. The central range, the cross-bar of the H, is faced in brick. The windows are bigger and more elaborate than they would have been originally, and two, towards the southern end of the wing, have friezes of small arches in the ornate Gothic Revival style of the nineteenth century. The south wing, the left-hand upright of the H, is also brick-faced and appears to date also to the nineteenth century, but in both cases the brick walls conceal an ancient framework of timber, suggesting that these parts of the house go back centuries further.

The closely spaced timbers of the Old Grammar School show this to be a building constructed to a high specification, in the best tradition of Midlands carpentry.

But the real gem is the north wing, because here the timber frame is still exposed, and displays carpentry of the highest status. This frame is close-studded, in other words the timber uprights, or studs, are placed very close together – often so close that the gaps between are narrower than the timbers on either side of them. So whoever built this house had access to a plentiful supply of timber, a costly building material, and was keen to show off this fact.

Another high-status aspect of the building is the way in which the upper floor protrudes beyond the line of the wall below, a feature known as a jetty. Jetties provided useful extra floor space upstairs. They also required extra timber and painstaking carpentry to make them structurally sound. For this reason, jetties were a sign of wealth and status. Many town houses only had a jetty at the front, so that the owner could show off to passers-by. But at the Saracen's Head there are jetties all around the north wing – a true example of conspicuous consumption.

Looking closely at the jetty, one can see what a large quantity of timber was needed to build a house like this. Where the floor of the upper storey is built out above the lower, the row of joists stick out, and their ends are clearly visible – each one runs right across the building. Then above the joists is a long horizontal timber called the bressummer, which acts as a sort of sill for the upper wall, reinforcing the structure and holding it together. At the corner, where two jetties meet, still more

Timbers lean, apparently precariously, on brick at the Saracen's Head. The variations in the colour and surface texture of the bricks suggest alterations at different periods.

The pronounced jetty, or overhanging upper storey, is a feature of the Saracen's Head that marks it as a high-status building.

reinforcement is needed, this time provided by a strong upright, called a dragon post, and a projecting wooden bracket, called a dragon beam, which was often elaborately carved. You needed a lot of timber to achieve all this. And a lot of skill, too. In an era before convenient fixings such as screws, oak building frames were assembled by cutting mortise and tenon joints with a mallet and chisel, and holding these together with pegs of oak. So a building like the Saracen's Head is not merely a testament to the wealth of its builder, but also a memorial to the ability of the late-medieval carpenters who made and assembled its frame.

The likelihood is that this precious north wing was a house in its own right. The structure suggests that the layout was that of a typical late-medieval 'hall house'. A central large living room, the hall, was flanked at one end by a private room, the parlour, and at the other by a passage hidden from the hall by a screen. To the other side of this 'screens passage' were the service rooms of the house, the kitchen, pantry, and buttery. Above the main rooms were bedchambers, but the kitchen was topped by a 'smoke bay', a space above the fire through which the smoke passed to an opening in the roof.

The flattened Tudor-style arch, the small bricks, and the stone-framed windows suggest that the lower portion of the Grammar School wall is old, even though it was added after the original timber-framed structure was built.

With simple late-medieval oak furniture — trestle tables, benches, chests, beds — and tapestries on the walls, the interior would have been attractive and comfortable. But glass was an expensive luxury and even a wealthy house like this may well not have had glazed windows. Instead there may have been panels of oiled cloth stretched on wooden frames, to let in a little light while keeping out the worst of the wind. In addition, for extra warmth and security, there were wooden shutters. These shutters were opened and closed by sliding horizontally, and in the north wing a number of timbers with long grooves indicate that many of the windows were protected in this way. One can even find the position of former windows by seeking out the running grooves of sliding shutters.

These buildings demonstrate a history of lively use. The Saracen's Head is currently the parish office and the setting for community events such as choir practices. An old table in the Grammar School bears the imprint of generations of pupils in the form of deeply carved graffiti.

After a period as an inn the building was finally given to the church, which has used it as a parish office and meeting place. As Canon Morris explained, 'It is a great privilege to have this building so near to the church.' But it is also a challenge. The building does not meet modern standards of accessibility and the old parts need to be treated with care – modern use can put excessive strain on an ancient building.

The Old Grammar School offers a similar challenge. It is just as fascinating a building as its neighbour. Outside, it puts on a colourful face, with a mix of materials that show the ingenuity of the Warwickshire builders. The plinth is sandstone, the lower floor is walled in brick, and the tall upper floor is timber-framed with close-studding similar to that at the Saracen's Head. Looking more closely, one can see that these materials reveal the building's development. It was originally completely timber-framed, and some of the timbers in the upper floor have been dated to between 1434 and 1460. The lower brickwork sticks out from the line of the timber frame above, and this reveals it to be a later facing. It was added during the Elizabethan period. In addition, the upper floor contains a window with ornate tracery in the style of around 1340. Presumably this window was retained from an earlier building and installed when the fifteenth-century timber-framed structure was built.

So from the structure alone, one can see that this is a building with a long history. From documents, we know that its use as a school goes back a long way. The commissioners of Edward VI recorded it in 1548, noting that it was already in operation.

They approved of the master, and recommended that he should have wages of ten pounds a year. Their king was a Protestant, and no doubt the school was run on strict Protestant lines. It certainly was by the seventeenth century, when it enjoyed a golden period under one of the country's most respected schoolmasters, Thomas Hall. Thomas was a Puritan – he wrote tracts condemning decadent Cavalier fashions such as long hair and the wearing of make-up. He was also a rigorous teacher, attracting pupils from as far afield as Ireland, helping many of them to win places at his old university, Oxford, and amassing a large library.

As a Puritan and Protestant, Thomas supported Parliament in England's Civil War, but lived to see the monarchy restored when Charles II came to the throne in 1660. The new regime brought trouble for Thomas because, in 1662, all clergy were asked to subscribe universally to the Prayer Book and men like Thomas were required to renounce their Presbyterian faith in favour of Anglicanism. This Thomas felt he could not do and he became one of more than nine hundred clergy ejected from their posts. He died a sad man in 1665 and was buried amongst his parishioners in the churchyard near the Grammar School.

The school carried on after Thomas's death. It was still operating in the nineteenth century, but it seems that standards had slipped by then. Latin had disappeared from the curriculum, although the practicalities of reading, writing, and accounts were taught. The building was also deteriorating and there was a restoration in 1910 and more repairs in 1951. Now it is time for further work on both buildings. The plan is to adapt the Victorian parts of the Saracen's Head, making them more accessible and giving them the facilities needed for parish and community use. The medieval parts of the building can then be restored for uses that do not put too much strain on the fabric. Likewise the Old Grammar School, which could become a centre that schoolchildren can visit to find out how young people were educated in the time of Thomas Hall. The result, hopes Canon Morris, will be to make the best use of these magnificent buildings next to the church: 'The development of these buildings should be a spur to wider regeneration, ensuring that the church is open to the wider community and not set apart. In the end it is about restoring a life and vitality which should have been there all the time.'

The timbers are just as impressive inside as out – heavy oak braces tie together the roof structure of the Old Grammar School.

Bawdsey Radar Station

The invention of the aeroplane transformed warfare. By the 1930s, a squadron of bombers could flatten an entire city district, killing everyone in the path of their deadly armaments. The attackers could be on to their target with such speed that defence seemed impossible. The only way for one air force to beat another was to have more bombs and aircraft than their opponents because, as British Prime Minister Stanley Baldwin put it in 1932, 'The bomber will always get through.'

But soon a team of British scientists were leading the way out of this malaise. They developed existing technology to create radar, a system of detecting distant objects using radio waves, and radar stations were soon being built around Britain's coasts in preparation for the expected attack from Hitler's Germany. This ground-breaking work was done on the remote Suffolk coast, at Bawdsey.

One of the first to see the need for better defence systems against enemy aircraft was Henry Wimperis, a scientist working for the British Air Ministry, who set up the Committee for the Scientific Survey of Air Defence under the leadership of Sir Henry Tizard, eminent chemist and rector of Imperial College, London. One of the experts they contacted was physicist Robert Watson-Watt, who had come up with a method of detecting thunderstorms by picking up the radio waves they emit. Watson-Watt suggested that radio waves be bounced off aircraft, so that they too could be detected. By February 1935 the scientist had set up a demonstration, bouncing radio waves off a Handley-Page bomber and picking up the reflected signal. Some six weeks later the government made a grant of £12,300 to develop the system.

Bawdsey was the first radar station and the place where the system was developed and refined. The original research station was centred on a number of huts, which contained the transmitter laboratory and generator facilities. But it was dominated by 75-metre-tall towers that sent out the radio waves and picked up the reflections as they returned. These lattice-work structures must have looked completely alien on the flat Suffolk coast, but in this isolated spot few people knew that they were there or what they were for and Watson-Watt and his colleagues pursued their secretive research.

Mary Wain, of the Bawdsey Radar Group, pointed out that in spite of the importance of the work done here, the buildings have been neglected for years. The group has now been offered one of the most important buildings, the transmitter block, to restore. It hopes to restore this structure to a condition that will enable it to be opened to the public as a memorial to the work that was done here – and as a fascinating educational visitor attraction. Many people would be intrigued to learn about the vital work done in this quiet corner of Suffolk.

Many of the radar station's rooms are dark and empty. Here there is only the old sign from the base, which waits for the day when restoration is complete and it can be re-erected.

As Mary Wain pointed out, this was secret work, which was known to few people at the time and has still received too little recognition: 'Much of the work in the receiving stations was done by women, who made up about 18 per cent of the Air Force at this time. Now we are more aware of the amount women contributed to the war effort, it makes sense that we should recognise the work they did at Bawdsey.'

But radar soon spread much further afield. The air defence committee quickly realised that for this remarkable system to work, radar stations would have to be set up around the south and eastern coasts of England, from the Wash to the Isle of Wight, covering all the possible points of entry for enemy bombers coming from Europe. So they began work on a series of radar stations with even taller, 105-metre towers. The transmitter towers were made of steel, the receiver towers of wood, which prevented the towers themselves producing confusing 'ghost' radar images. The resulting network of stations became known as the Chain Home system, and it was one of

Solid, roughly finished poured concrete is the material of many of the buildings. It was valued both for its strength and for the way in which it enabled rapid construction – an essential factor when speed could save lives.

the vital elements in British air defence during World War II. Without it, the RAF could never have won the Battle of Britain against the vastly larger forces of the Luftwaffe.

Various specialist structures were needed for the site. The buildings needed to be erected quickly; they also needed to be strong, because Bawdsey would be a prime target if the enemy realised its importance to the defence of Britain. The obvious material was concrete. This could either be poured into moulds made on site, as it was to build the transmitter block that the Bawdsey Radar Group plans to restore; or it could be produced as prefabricated units and transported to the site for rapid construction. The strongest type of concrete was reinforced with steel rods, but strong walls could also be made with mass concrete and both types were used at Bawdsey.

These structures were not erected for their beauty. Where poured concrete was used, any available material might be used to make the shuttering that formed the mould – rough or

A heavy concrete trapdoor opens to reveal one of the underground rooms. Dark and cold now, this was once a scene of heated activity, and was all but invisible to enemy bombers in the sky above.

smooth timber, sheet steel, or corrugated metal could all be used. And the concrete itself could be mixed with pebbles from the nearby beach, large stones that did not make ideal aggregate (generally, the smaller the stones in the aggregate, the stronger the concrete), but they were easily obtainable, plentiful, and free.

The complex also includes 'soft' buildings, structures made of brick that are more vulnerable to attack. The builders tried a different way of protecting these structures. They are surrounded

As the years have passed rabbits have colonised the earth banks, eroding away defences that could originally withstand the bomb blasts.

by earth revetments supported by reinforced concrete walls.
These barriers originally sloped smoothly, the idea being to
direct the force of an explosion up and over the buildings within.
The banks are now somewhat depleted, as the result of the local
rabbit population, burrowing away for some sixty years.

This system gave sideways protection but would have left the
buildings open to bombs dropped from above if they did not
have extra-strong roofs. So these blocks are roofed with a 'skin' of
reinforced concrete, topped with a two-foot layer of beach
shingle, topped with a further reinforced-concrete skin. The idea
was that if there was a direct hit from overhead, even if the roof
itself was damaged, the building below would survive intact. To
reduce the likelihood of an attack, however, the roofs were
painted with bitumen to help them blend into their surroundings
– and to keep out water, which otherwise would have penetrated
the concrete and made the reinforcing rods rusty and weak.

Among the site's other special structures was a large 400-gallon
tank beneath the transmitter room. This held distilled water, which
was used to cool the valves that generated the radio frequencies
required for radar. In the days before transistors or microchips, all

electronic equipment, from radios
and TV sets to early radar and
computer devices, relied on valves,
which produced a large amount of
heat. At Bawdsey there was another
way of getting rid of the hot air
produced by the valves. Two ducts
ran out of the building and under
the earth revetments, and traces of
them may still remain on site.

Since the station closed,
much of the original
radar equipment has
disappeared, although
some later equipment is
stored in some of the
buildings. This often
happens in empty
buildings, and poses a
challenge to curators
when they come to
assess which items to
keep and how to
conserve them.

The complex at Bawdsey took a terrific effort to create –
effort both in the research of the scientists and in the labour of
the builders. Well aware of the site's vulnerability, the
authorities ordered the station to be surrounded by a
minefield, and various measures, such as rubber door seals and
air locks, to be provided to safeguard against gas attacks. They
also installed duplicate equipment, so that the station could
carry on functioning if one area was destroyed in an air raid.
But as the war went on, the provisions went even further. Two
other radar stations, at Ventnor on the Isle of Wight and

Wartling near Bexhill in Sussex, were hit by German bombers. So as a last resort, in case both the above-ground facilities at Bawdsey were attacked, they also installed a reserve system underground. This consisted of a low-budget version of the main equipment, but it was buried under about three metres of soil and was virtually impregnable.

Bawdsey survived at least a dozen German attacks, from various bombs to a V2 rocket which missed its target and ended up in the sea. It is now one of the few Chain Home stations to survive – appropriately, in view of its pivotal role in the early

RESTORATION Update Midlands and East Anglia News from the first series

There was a lot of public interest in Stoke's Bethesda Chapel after its appearance on *Restoration*, with extensive coverage in both the local and national press and on local radio. A committee has been formed to raise funds and offer other support, and people have come forward with photographs of the building at different stages in its history which will be helpful when restoration can begin. An Audience Development Plan has been completed, to identify potential uses for the chapel that respect its historic fabric. Emergency repairs have been carried out and security has been improved. But the building is still very fragile and substantial funding is needed quickly to save it from further deterioration.

At Newman Brothers' Coffin Furniture Factory the Regional Development Agency, Advantage West Midlands, have backed the building by buying it, together with its unique contents. They have also indicated that further funding, up to a total of £1.3 million, is likely to be available, subject to a full application and match funding being in place. Meanwhile, there has been a high attendance at open days, with a pleasingly wide range of ages, from teenage Goths to elderly former workers, enjoying the factory. The arrival of one ex-employee, who sat down in her old place of work and began to explain everything she used to do, alerted the building's custodians to an invaluable historical resource – the stories of those who worked here. One project for which funding is being sought is therefore a scheme to film former Newmans' employees explaining and reminiscing about their working lives.

development of the radar technology. It may look unassuming – indeed its buildings were designed to be difficult to see – but it played a key role in World War II. Locally, there is already plenty of recognition of this and support for the restoration project. Mary Wain pointed to a recent open day: 'We expected about 50 visitors, but around 900 turned up. And thousands – up to 180,000 a year – come to the Bawdsey area. Many of them would be keen to come to the radar station and discover its role in the war.' As a reminder of a vital technological development that helped the RAF's airmen to victory in their defence of Britain's skies, Bawdsey's transmitter block richly deserves to be restored.

Greyfriars Tower is to get its restoration, thanks to funding from the Heritage Lottery Fund, English Heritage, and King's Lynn and West Norfolk Council. The plan is to restore the thirteenth-century friary tower and landscape the tower gardens. This will make the tower accessible to visitors once more, as well as providing interpretation to help visitors understand the building. It is hoped that work will begin in November 2004 and be completed just under twelve months later.

It is also good news at Moulton Windmill – restoration is already under way and the completion of the first and principal phase is due in spring 2005. By this time it is hoped that the mill's tower and cap will be fully restored and that the machinery will all be in place. The downstairs granary area will be refurbished and facilities such as public toilets installed, with full disabled access to the first and second floors. The granary area will be available for people to hire for functions, while there will be an exhibition space on the first floor. Meanwhile, funding is being sought for the second phase – the restoration of the sails and gallery. A sponsorship scheme is already in place through which one can fund a shutter and get the mill closer to the £250,000 needed to complete the project.

The custodians of Coalhouse Fort in Essex are working on the planning needed to make a successful bid for funding. They are looking at the fort's management and at ways of making it sustainable in the future. Since *Restoration* they have enjoyed a higher profile, which has brought not only many visitors but also two separate film companies seeking to use the site as a location for a documentary about World War II and for the latest Batman movie.

RESTORATION

THE NORTH

Sheffield Manor Lodge SHEFFIELD

Gayle Mill HAWES

Lion Salt Works NORTHWICH

The North of England is a region of contrasts, of almost empty countryside and great conurbations, of hills and dales, of agriculture and industry. It encompasses many different areas, from the Lake District to the North York Moors, the Cheviot Hills to the Forest of Bowland, all distinctive in scenery and history. It is impossible to generalise about the North, yet its people have often stood together in their separateness from the rest of the country, and politicians and commentators still talk about a 'North–South divide'.

United in their diversity, the communities of the North have made huge contributions to the life of Britain as a whole. In the Middle Ages and the Tudor period their distance from London did not prevent them from playing major political roles – after all, the northernmost regions such as Northumberland were in the front line in English relations with the Scots. And northern industry has been hugely important in building the wealth of the nation. The role of cotton towns like Manchester in the industrial revolution is well known. But the industrial prowess of the North goes back much further than this in its dealing with more home-grown commodities, such as salt and wool.

The three restoration candidates from the North of England are all involved in the long-standing power and influence of the region. The earliest is Sheffield Manor Lodge, a Tudor

The Turret House at Manor Lodge in Sheffield is a typical Elizabethan structure, which may well have been designed by leading architect of the time, Robert Smythson.

mansion mostly in ruins but with one important standing building. The home of one of the richest families of the Elizabethan period, it demonstrates first of all how the Tudor rulers extended the power of their court far from London into the shires. This was the beginning of the heyday of the country house, when grandees like the Earl of Shrewsbury, the owner of Manor Lodge, set up virtual satellites of the court in the provinces. Not for nothing have these buildings been called 'power houses'. But more than this, Manor Lodge was the place where Mary, Queen of Scots was held prisoner in the 1570s and 1580s, so it also has its place in the troubled story of Anglo-Scottish relations in the sixteenth century.

The other two northern candidates represent the region's unparalleled industrial history. Gayle Mill was built at a turning point in the long history of textile production in the North. Large parts of Yorkshire had been wool country for centuries. Cistercian monks, for example, had come here in the Middle Ages and farmed sheep on a huge scale. At the beginning of the industrial revolution, far-sighted merchants and mill-owners began to turn to a new, imported fibre, cotton. Gayle is one of the earliest factories built for cotton-working, and one of very few to survive. In addition, it has an interesting later history. When the profits from spinning took a downturn, the building began a new life as a sawmill. Much of the machinery from this industry is still in place, allowing us to see that one of the

interesting things about a building is often how its use changed over the years.

The remaining candidate also served a long-standing industry. The Lion Salt Works was purpose-built for the production of salt by evaporation, a business with a history that stretches back to the Romans at least. Unlike Gayle Mill, the salt works continued to fulfil its original role, with salt being produced until 1986. This is remarkable, since its buildings seem very fragile – they are mostly timber-framed structures that look as if they were designed for a short life. But in fact they were well adapted for their use. Timber was a good material to withstand the high humidity caused by the evaporation process and to cope with the subsidence that was endemic in the early days of salt-working. The timber-framed structures of the Lion Works stood up to these tests, serving as shining examples of how a local building style was well suited to a specialist use.

So all three northern buildings were part of much larger networks – diplomatic and court networks linking to Sheffield Manor Lodge, canals taking cotton from Gayle to the ports and cities, and roads, some of them the most ancient of tracks, taking salt from Cheshire all over the country. Now they are united in their need, and their custodians hope that the networks forged by conservationists and television companies will give them the support they richly deserve.

Gayle Mill sits in a fold of the Yorkshire Dales. A derelict tripod crane hints at the survival of other machinery inside.

The Lion Salt Works was sited next to the Trent and Mersey Canal, so that fuel could be delivered and salt dispatched with ease.

Sheffield Manor Lodge

The Elizabethans were some of the most prolific builders of large houses. Queen Elizabeth herself built little, but her courtiers vied with each other to create the most lavish houses where, with a mixture of hope and trepidation, they waited for a visit from the sovereign – hope, because a royal visit conferred prestige and influence; trepidation because royal households were so huge that the expense of putting them up could be crippling.

One couple who were successful in the Elizabethan building boom were the Earl of Shrewsbury, one of the most senior peers of the time, and his wife Elizabeth, known most widely as Bess of Hardwick, a Derbyshire squire's daughter who by a series of astute dynastic marriages had become the richest woman in England after the queen. Bess owned several houses in her own right, including the lavish Hardwick Hall in Derbyshire. The earl's main home was Sheffield Castle, but his forebears had also built Manor Lodge, a more comfortable home nearby.

Manor Lodge was a grand house, sited on a hill. An account of 1637 described it as 'fairly built with stone and timber, with an inward court and an outward court, two gardens, and three yards'. But the owners left it in the seventeenth century for their estates in southern England, and most of the building is now an extensive set of ruins, some one or two storeys high, some with cellars beneath. The one exception is a building known as the Turret House, probably first built as a gatehouse, which stands four-square and solid as a reminder of what the whole must once have been like.

But Clare Dykes, project manager for the site, explained that the Turret House is not quite as solid as it looks. 'The roof is fairly sound, but needs work. In one of the upper rooms, damp has brought much of the plaster ceiling down. In the room next door, the ceiling is also deteriorating. This is original plasterwork from 1574.' This important building clearly needs attention before the damage gets worse.

Manor Lodge is remarkable in two ways. First, the Turret House was built when additions were made to the main house in 1574, and may well be the work of the great Elizabethan architect Robert Smythson, who was later to design Hardwick

The Turret House is a simple, four-square stone building, set off with carefully designed details such as the string courses (the stone bands that run horizontally around the walls) and the doorway with its flattened Tudor arch.

Hall for Bess. Second, the house was one of the places where Mary, Queen of Scots was imprisoned when, as a Catholic ruler, she acted as a focus for opponents to Queen Elizabeth I. These men threatened to topple Elizabeth and place her rival on the English throne.

Next to the row of chimneys, a small turret like a pepperpot gives access to the flat roof.

In fact, the Shrewsbury family had a track record as hosts to those in trouble with the Crown. In 1530, Cardinal Wolsey stayed at Manor Lodge for fifteen days en route to London to answer a charge of treason. The tower where he lodged survives, together with its impressive two-storey garderobe, or lavatory. In Wolsey's time the tower was described as new, and it seems likely that the Shrewsburys made many additions to the house, making it larger and more lavish as the sixteenth century went on.

Building was still ongoing in the 1570s, and by this time the Turret House was under construction. A four-square stone building with large windows and battlements, it has survived its four hundred years rather well. It is a plain, solid structure, with

The ornate stained glass dates from the restoration of the Turret House in 1872, but its heraldic symbols are in keeping with the building's history.

battlements and a flat roof, the one ornate external detail being a round stair turret sticking up above the parapet and giving access to the roof. Its similarity to other buildings by Smythson, and Smythson's connection to Bess, make it likely that he was the architect of the Turret House.

Why was the Turret House built? There is a long tradition that it was designed to house Mary, Queen of Scots. The Victorians certainly thought so, and installed commemorative stained glass when they restored the building. But even as a prisoner Mary would have been accompanied by a large staff, and would have lived in some luxury, surrounded by the best tapestries and sleeping in the finest linen. The Turret House seems too small for her and her retinue.

Some of the ruins stand quite high, giving a good idea of the size of the main house.

It is more likely that the Turret House was built for entertainment, as a kind of grandstand from which the earl and his guests could watch the hunting in the nearby park, admiring the view from the roof or from one of the rooms below, and enjoying rich feasts. This kind of use for such a building was not unusual in the late sixteenth century and Smythson designed a similar building for the family, known as the Stand or the Hunting Tower, at their house at Chatsworth in Derbyshire.

And yet the building does seem to insist on its links with the Scottish queen. Inside, the ornate plasterwork of the ceiling incorporates Mary's emblem, a marigold turned to face the sun, as well as the earl's coat of arms, Talbot dogs (his family name was Talbot), and the family motto. Still more tellingly, the plasterwork includes a design showing a hand grasping a spray of flowers by the stems, an emblem of the loss of freedom. So it seems likely that Mary used this room at some time, or was brought here to be reminded, as if she needed a reminder, of her curtailed freedom. Either that, or the earl was simply keen to use the interior decoration of his house as a way of pointing out his loyalty to Queen Elizabeth.

But there were rumours that this loyalty was tainted. With Bess away at Chatsworth, it was said that the earl and the Queen of Scots began an affair. When Bess heard the rumour, she wrote to her husband enclosing some lettuce, which was meant to cool his lust. But the Shrewsburys' marriage did not rekindle its former warmth and the couple stayed apart. Mary left the earl's care in 1584. Three years later, Elizabeth finally bowed to pressure and had the Scottish queen executed. By 1590 Shrewsbury, beset by black moods, had also died. The heyday of Manor Lodge was over.

The next earl died in 1616 and the property passed to the Dukes of Norfolk, who deserted it in favour of their estates in Sussex. Abandoned and pillaged for building materials, the house gradually decayed. In the nineteenth century, part of the park was used to build housing for the poor. A coal mine was sunk behind the tower that had once housed Cardinal Wolsey. But the Victorians did restore the one solid standing building, the Turret House, ensuring that it has survived intact until today. The building remains, adjacent to the ruins and near to a pair of housing estates, an uneasy juxtaposition of old and new, rich and poor.

The ruins next to the tower still give some idea of the extent and grandeur of the original house. The main courtyard, divided into two parts, can still be made out, as can the excavated remains of a cellar. One range contains the long gallery, which was on the upper floor – the use of the room below it is not known. The ruins of Wolsey's tower still stand, and the chimneys, fireplaces, and remains of the garderobes within give a hint of the kind of comfort that was expected in the mansion of a Tudor grandee. These rooms would once have been just as luxurious as those in the Turret House.

For some decades the site has been leased by the local council, and their stewardship has ensured that Turret House has been kept secure and weatherproof. An archaeological dig in the 1960s helped to reveal much about the history and structure of the ruins, and occasional open days have given visitors access to the site.

It is the aim of the Trust that now cares for Manor Lodge to conserve the remains, open them more regularly, and make it easier for visitors to appreciate the relationship between the ruins and the Turret House. Clare Dykes explained some of the plans for the site. 'The Turret House needs its roof repaired and conservation work done on the interior. Then it should be possible to add furnishings to give an impression of how the interiors might have looked in 1574. Finds from the digs on the site could also be displayed.' To help people appreciate the ruins, the plan is to install a high-level walkway, at the height of the old long gallery, so that one can see the remains clearly and understand the ground plan of the house. The ruins themselves will be conserved and a visitors' centre will eventually be constructed.

But Clare Dykes was also keen to explain the wider context. 'The house is part of a much larger site, including various farm buildings. The plan is to convert some of these structures to create an education centre and a centre for training in heritage skills.' If this is achieved, the site will bring huge benefits to Sheffield – the conservation of a valuable green space, job opportunities, the chance to learn about the past and its care, and the opportunity to see the sort of living conditions enjoyed by the Shrewsburys, and the queen who was their captive guest.

As in many Tudor buildings, a mixture of stone blocks, rubble, and bricks was used.

Gayle Mill

When visitors come to the Yorkshire Dales they see first of all the natural beauty of the area – the hills, valleys, and streams. But, like most of the English landscape, the Dales retain the indelible imprint of human activity, especially the centuries-old activity of sheep farming. But this rural area has also been industrial for centuries, with home-working spinners and weavers playing a key part in the local economy.

In the eighteenth century one family who were immersed in this industrial culture were the Rouths of Gayle, near Hawes. Oswald and Thomas Routh were hosiers, men who would 'put out' their wool to a small army of independent hand-knitters who produced garments – especially hosiery – for the Rouths to sell. The Rouths were wool men through and through, but in the 1770s they embarked on a different venture – cotton. They built Gayle Mill, possibly on the site of a former corn mill, as the heart of their new business.

Cotton was the new material of the period, and offered the industrialist the chance of riches. Pioneer factory-owner Richard Arkwright had invented the water frame, a water-

powered spinning machine, in 1769. Large-scale mechanical spinning of cheap imported cotton seemed the way to go and cotton was soon overtaking wool as Britain's leading textile industry. Oswald and Thomas followed Arkwright's lead. Indeed, as Graham Bell, of the North East Civic Trust, explained, Arkwright may have provided the template for the mill's design: 'It was designed like a machine, to fit the machinery that was going to be installed there.' By the late 1770s, the well-oiled machine was in production.

The mill stands by the stream that gave it its power. It is built on a slope so that one side has three storeys while on the other there are two. The walls are built of solid local stone, the roof is slate, and each floor has rows of windows, generously proportioned to let in the light. Its local materials and its position on the sloping ground help the mill blend into the surrounding countryside, a typical example of the industrial vernacular architecture of this part of Yorkshire. But not everyone saw it that way. Visitor John Byng, arriving in 1792, resented the intrusion of industry into the countryside. Byng complained that 'prospect and quiet are destroy'd' and that 'With the bell ringing, and the clamour of the mill, all the vale is disturb'd.' But the Rouths were not going to let a little extra noise stand in their way.

The millpond wall is one of the surviving parts of the system that topped up the mill's water supply when the flow in the stream was weak.

An arch crowns a water outlet in a building in which water and stone seem at one.

This noisy machinery did several different jobs that had previously been managed by hand. A carding engine, another recent invention of Arkwright's, was used to comb out and untangle the cotton fibres. A roving machine evened and extended the slivers of fibre. Spinning was done on water frames, heavy machines that vibrated continuously and were therefore placed on the ground floor of the mill. It was state of the art, and, like other mill owners of the time, the Rouths hoped it would make them a lot of money.

The brothers built themselves a handsome house, but things did not go as smoothly as they had planned. Like many early cotton mills, Gayle did not do as well as hoped. One reason was probably that the early machinery was not very reliable. Textile-working technology was developing very quickly at this time, with better-made, more dependable machines being introduced all the time. It does not always pay to be a pioneer, installing almost experimental, but also temperamental, equipment. The rural setting of the business did not help either. In spite of the Richmond to Lancaster turnpike road, which brought cotton into the area, it would have been easier to set up in one of the large towns nearer the coast. Mills in such locations, with their lower transport costs, tended to do better

A channel some 300 metres in length delivered water from the millpond. One aspect of the restoration project here is to conserve this remarkable water-delivery system.

than the rural mills. So, in 1789, the brothers tried to sell or lease the mill at Gayle. But they found no takers and instead tried other solutions, spinning flax, and later returning to the business they knew best, hosiery. Finally they leased it to another hosier, one E. A. Knowles, but by 1840 the mill was closed and empty.

No one knows for sure how the mill was used in the mid-nineteenth century; it may have remained unoccupied for several decades. But in the late 1870s it began a new lease of life as a sawmill. A new vortex water turbine was installed to power the sawyer's machinery and soon the timber was arriving. Great tree trunks were cut into planks on the ground floor before the wood was taken upstairs and made into a range of goods – especially equipment such as carts, hay sledges, and hay rakes – that were bought by the local farming community. In common with many joiners – in the Victorian period and well into the twentieth century – the Aldersons,

When an extra-long tree trunk had to be sawn, the end could stick out of a window, resting on this wooden support.

the family who ran the sawmill, also acted as the local undertakers. They prospered and the sawmill continued in operation until 1988, when changes in the timber and joinery businesses forced them to close, leaving a question mark over the future of Gayle Mill.

From quite soon after its closure it was clear that Gayle Mill was an important building in a number of ways. As Graham Bell explained, only a handful of cotton mills were built in this area, and few have survived as intact as Gayle. So it has huge local significance as evidence of a key phase in the history of this part of Yorkshire. In addition, the building is an archetypal

Among the remaining confusion of wooden and steel fixtures are a bench with a vice by a window (above) and an extended bench fitted with a circular saw (right), showing that the mill could handle sizeable timbers.

early cotton mill – its shape and size show the influence of Arkwright's own mill at Cromford in Derbyshire (itself featured in the previous series of *Restoration*). And there is the additional history of the building as a water-powered sawmill – this alone would make it a rare survival.

Gayle preserves valuable remains of its time as both a cotton mill and a sawmill, and this is one of the things that make it unique. The stone walls with their well-cut quoins at the corners, the slate roof framed by a stone parapet at the gables, the rows of windows, and the riverside setting, make it a typical rural cotton mill. The early turbine, made by Williamson of

Rusting corrugated iron and crumbling stone walls pose a challenge for the mill's custodians.

Kendal, together with a later turbine and a quantity of woodworking machinery, are testimony to the building's sawmill phase. The main circular saw is still in situ on the building's lower floor, positioned so that it could cope with trees as long as the building – they could even extend its operation outside one of the windows if necessary. Smaller woodworking machinery is still installed on the floor above.

Side by side these varied remains, of cotton- and woodworking and of different types of power source, stand for another kind of significance. They speak eloquently of the ingenuity of the owners in their efforts to make the building self-sufficient, using the most efficient form of energy that could be generated from the local water supply. So they began with a water wheel to power the water frame, progressed to the water turbine to drive the mechanical saws, and ended with another turbine that generated hydro-electricity to power both a new generation of electric woodworking machinery and the local street lighting. As those associated with the building like to say, it was always at the cutting edge of technology.

Graham Bell pointed out that the power-generation machinery is a very special survival: 'Machines like these, which can be restored so that they can work once again, are very rare survivors. They are at the heart of our plans to make Gayle a working mill once more.' There has already been much progress in raising funds for the project, but more money is needed, especially for the mill's unique water system.

The restoration plans acknowledge the whole history of the mill. When open as a tourist attraction, the building's roles as both cotton mill and sawmill will be explained and interpreted. But, in the spirit in which the mill has always been run, the Trust hopes to make Gayle sustainable by reviving its use as a working timber mill. Training in timberwork, forest management, and allied skills will be provided as part of a recognised course, possibly with a local college. Such a scheme would allow the mill to play a key role in the forestry industry of the Dales, while providing opportunities for local young people to train in an industry in which they would have a good chance of finding a job locally.

In addition, the mill will produce timber products for sale, perhaps functional but well-made items such as stiles and gates for parks and gardens. Market research has shown that there is demand locally for well-crafted items of this type, and once the products are established, the market could expand. There is already considerable interest in the project, both locally and farther afield.

Visitors will be welcome at the restored Gayle Mill and the Trust intends to show them the building's unique history as both a textile and timber mill. People who come here will be impressed by this long history and by the way local workers process local timber using power from the local stream. And so they will appreciate once more how human industry and nature can combine successfully in this beautiful part of the country.

Lion Salt Works

We take salt for granted today. But in past times it was a scarce and precious commodity, as is indicated by a number of English phrases using salt to indicate value or status. 'The salt of the earth', 'worth his salt', 'above the salt' – they all show that the substance was valued to former generations. And places where salt was produced, such as the famous Cheshire 'salt towns' of Nantwich, Middlewich, and Northwich, grew prosperous through the business of extracting salt using the open-pan process. The Lion Salt Works in Northwich is the only place where all the equipment, machinery, and buildings used in this process remain.

The works are silent now. Henry Thompson, former part-owner of the complex who worked there from 1947 until the closure in 1986, would like to see this change: 'It is sad to see buildings like this, that have been the scene of so much activity, silent and empty. I would be delighted if they could be restored so that people could see how important this industry once was in Cheshire.'

Salt working was established in Cheshire because of the natural sources of 'wild brine', salt water that could be pumped up from subterranean beds of rock salt and heated in pans so that the liquid evaporated to leave salt crystals behind. The industry had been present in Cheshire for centuries. Even before the Romans arrived, brine was being taken from natural springs.

But the salt business really took off in the eighteenth century, in parallel with the coal industry. Steam-driven pumps, developed to extract water from coal mines, were equally useful for raising brine to the surface. And coal was an ideal fuel for heating the salt pans, especially after the rise of the iron industry, which was increasingly taking the alternative, wood, to make charcoal to fire its blast furnaces. So the Cheshire salt towns boomed, along with Liverpool and the northern coalfields. Coal was sent into Cheshire along the Trent and Mersey Canal. Salt was sent back and, once it arrived at the great port on the Mersey, could be exported all over the world.

Heavily corroded machinery still stands inside a rather lightweight structure of timber walls and roofs at the Lion Salt Works.

The salt works' source
of heat survives in the
shape of a row of
furnaces. There is plenty
of evidence of salt
deposits on their
brickwork.

The Thompson family of Marston, near Northwich, had been involved in the salt industry at least since the 1720s. John Thompson and his son Henry Ingram Thompson sank a mine at Marston in 1894, and this developed into the Lion Salt Works, named after the nearby Red Lion Hotel. Soon a sizeable complex of buildings covered the site, and the Thompsons were transporting salt on their own fleet of barges or on their own railway wagons, which could pull into a specially built siding. It was a serious business operation, and salt from the Lion Works was exported as far afield as the USA, Canada, Guatemala, India, Nigeria, and South Africa.

All the buildings used for this highly specialised work were purpose-built at the Lion Works. Many of these are timber-framed, and there are several reasons for this. For one thing, there was a strong tradition of timber building in Cheshire, stretching back over hundreds of years. For another, it was believed that wood would withstand the humidity involved in the salt-producing process better than other materials. Thirdly, timber responded better than brickwork to the corrosive action of the salt crystals. As Henry Thompson observed, 'At the Lion Salt Works, you won't find a right angle in the place. Both the heat and the crystallising salt have pushed everything out of true.' But at least the structure did not crack and crumble as a masonry building might have done. Finally, a timber-framed building was the best solution available in the nineteenth century to a besetting problem of the salt industry – subsidence. The removal of millions of gallons of brine from under the ground caused the rock and soil above to move. Buildings shifted as a result, producing all sorts of leans and cracks that once made the buildings of Northwich famously 'drunken'. A badly subsiding brick building will crack and eventually fall apart. A timber-framed structure, on the other hand, can be 'jacked up' to keep it level over the heaving ground. As a result, timber was the building material of choice for the salt-makers of Cheshire.

So an impressive number of the original buildings at the Lion Salt Works are still standing. There is the brine pump with its steam-driven 'nodding donkey' that brought the salt water to the surface, the great tank where the brine was stored, and, at the heart of the complex, the pan houses.

Building Preservation Trust member Andrew Fielding wields a skimmer, a perforated, ladle-like tool used to lift the crystals of salt from the pan.

It was in these pan houses that the brine was heated in large metal pans. Each pan was set over a fire in front of a brickwork flue that took away the fumes. Excess heat also travelled along the flues and was used to warm the adjacent hot houses, where the salt was dried. The pan houses were so full of steam that workers found it hard to see more than a foot or two in front of their faces. In the hot, stifling atmosphere most workers stripped to the waist – this had the added advantage of reducing the abrasive effect of the salt in the air, which could be uncomfortable if you wore a shirt. Each worker fired his own pan by hand, adding coal to control the temperature of the fire. Keeping a close eye on the brine in the pan, he would watch the salt crystals forming as a crust on the surface before they fell to the bottom as another crust began to form. The worker took a rake and drew the crystals to the side of the vessel before scooping them up and depositing them in the elm buckets that were arranged on an iron support running around the edge of the pan. Once the buckets were full and the excess brine had been drained away and recycled, the salt in the buckets would solidify into lumps of crystals. These lumps were turned out of the buckets like sandcastles on a beach and taken into the hot house to dry.

Old timbers, corrugated iron, and a lack of right angles – the buildings at the Lion Salt Works present further difficulties to the restorer.

Lumps usually spent eight days in the hot house drying out, after which they could be crushed to produce dry powder salt, cut into small lumps to give 'cut lump salt', or sold complete as 'bar salt'. Some form of airtight packing was preferred to keep out the moisture and stop the salt getting damp – both greaseproof paper and tins were used in the nineteenth century.

Remains of five pan houses survive at the Lion Salt Works. Those still in use in the 1960s were converted from coal to oil firing, which reduced running costs but gave less control over the heat than a coal fire tended by a skilled operator. Another interesting survival is the smithy, where the iron pans were made and repaired. The manager's office, another timber-framed structure, remains, as do the brine pump and the nearby iron tank, which could hold 30,000 gallons of brine and fed all the pans by gravity. Together, the group makes a unique survival, a fascinating memorial to the industrial heritage of north-western England.

There were always problems working in this industry. The humid atmosphere around the pans was uncomfortable and

Metal signs warn eloquently how far afield the salt vapours could spread, affecting not just the workers but those who passed nearby.

Many metal structures, such as tanks and pans, survive, but these corroding structures are a conservation challenge.

the damp made the floor slippery, leading to accidents in the pan houses. Then there was the unpleasantness caused by fumes when heaps of clinker caught fire in the yards around the works. In Victorian times, workers also had to put up with the moral attacks of critics who could not understand how men could strip to the waist in an industry that often brought them close to members of the opposite sex. Yet, as Henry Thompson pointed out, the vapour and heat created an atmosphere that was healthy in many ways. 'The salt acted as an antiseptic and on the whole it was a healthy life. And no one on the site was overweight!'

Above all, the salt trade was profitable enough to keep the business going through most of the twentieth century, and the skilled 'lumpmen' were well enough paid to make it worth their while to do long hours, often staying overnight to make sure their fires were properly tended. And so the business continued until 1986, when a declining market for salt in Africa, until then one of the major importers, finally made it unprofitable.

It leaves behind a group of buildings, together with tools and equipment, that represent a vital part of the economy of the last two centuries, and it is fitting that such rare survivals should be preserved. A start has already been made, in that the buildings are now owned by the local authority, the Vale Royal Borough Council, and administered by a charitable trust.

But preservation is a challenge. The fragile timber-framed buildings, which were never intended to be permanent

structures, now need thorough repairs. This is the first goal that the site's custodians need to achieve, before turning the complex into a working industrial museum, demonstrating salt production by the old method, but extracting the brine in a more modern and environmentally friendly way than that used by their

RESTORATION Update North
News from the first series

At Harperley Prisoner-of-War Camp the task of applying for funding for feasibility studies and other preliminary work is under way. The owners have opened eight of the huts, and the many visitors have been fascinated by the guided tours. As well as the increased public profile, the owners are thankful to *Restoration* for putting them in contact with specialists who are advising on the often complex business of making applications for funding.

Bank Hall has enjoyed a huge increase in visitor numbers since appearing in the series. On one afternoon alone 760 people arrived, compared with an annual figure of around 5,000 in previous years. This represents considerable local support for the house as well as great interest nationally. A funding bid to the Heritage Lottery Fund has been made and the result is eagerly awaited. But there is still a concern that the house is deteriorating rapidly – with every week, action becomes more and more urgent to save this fragile structure and to find an end-use that ensures public access.

Major advances are being made at the 700-acre Wentworth estate, where the conservatory and mock ruined castle were featured in the first series of *Restoration*. An extensive four-year programme of restoration and conservation is now in progress across the estate, with work planned on many of the twenty-six listed monuments. The castle will benefit from this work, in which the aim is to preserve it as a picturesque ruin and make its structure safe. The project does not include the restoration of the conservatory, but its custodians will make sure that its condition does not deteriorate further – they plan to raise money for its conservation in a future phase. They are grateful for the estate's coverage on *Restoration*, which helped to bring many individuals and organisations together behind the project.

nineteenth-century predecessors. They hope to open the buildings to the public, starting with the first pan house to be completed and gradually extending access to the whole site. Plenty of people in Cheshire and beyond are already keen to find out about this special reminder of their industrial heritage.

The winner of the first series of *Restoration* was Manchester's Victoria Baths, which impressed viewers both because of its stunning tiled interior and because of the special role it has played in the local community, providing both swimming and bathing facilities for much of the twentieth century. The £3.4 million raised by the series is to be spent on refurbishing the Turkish Baths, on which work is due to start next year. To the outsider this may seem a long way away, but when public money funds a project of this nature every plan has to be scrutinised – and that includes not just the architect's plans but studies covering every aspect of the building and the work, from how the precious tiles and threatened structure will be preserved to how the building will be used and made accessible. Meanwhile, the project team at the baths are looking at ways of raising the £20 million or so that will be needed to restore the rest of the complex.

Everyone involved with Ravensworth Castle has been pleased by the number of people who have come forward – from as far afield as Australia – since the series was broadcast, their memories and knowledge of the property often bringing information to light that was unknown to those nearer at hand. This has partly been the result of a campaign website, which, together with much local publicity, has built on the increased profile established by the *Restoration* series. Meanwhile, funding has been secured for a conservation plan and the owner is also carrying out a business review of the estate. When these studies are complete it is hoped that a decision will be made quickly about the castle's future – either with a commercially viable use that is sensitive to the historic fabric, or a subsidised restoration.

As a result of being featured on *Restoration*, Brackenhill Tower has now found a new private owner who plans to undertake the restoration work needed to save the building for future generations. The future of the tower seems secure.

PTOLEMY DEAN

A 'ruin detective's' perspective

I have never much cared for the term 'ruin detective', but when the first series of *Restoration* began we could not think of an alternative that explained more succinctly what we did. It was a most unusual privilege to be invited by a television company to look at ruins. All too often one has seen those sad, weed-strewn driveways that lead to an inevitably high fence, beyond which slumps the imprisoned silhouette of an ancient building engulfed by ivy and rot. I have always found myself consumed by curiosity to discover what lies within. What secrets of a long-forgotten history await the bulldozer? In the past one may have sought to gain entry through some breach in the defences (usually found around the back). But on *Restoration* the padlock to the main gate had already been opened and the heavy chain swung limply in the air. Marianne and I just strolled in.

Of course there were drawbacks. There was a film crew with us and they needed to capture the 'moment of discovery'. In the first series of *Restoration* we were expected to guess what the building was, in addition to its age and importance. Sometimes this was not immediately obvious – and silence ensued, much to the television makers' disappointment. This time we were better prepared, although the

research assistants, brimming with freshly gleaned information, were often reluctant to divulge too much. It was, after all, for us to 'discover'. Consequently we set off as we pleased, and the cameraman, cameraman's assistant, sound man (attached to the camera by a wire), and the coterie of researchers and producers could be heard thrashing their way through the brambles behind us. For directors used to strict control this must have come as quite a shock. But their revenge came in the edit suite when comments that one later regretted found their way into the films.

In the inevitable moments of delay while extra lights were fixed up, doors were unblocked, and health and safety audits checked, a quick sketch might emerge. This proved to be a soothing and rewarding process that gave time to look at the buildings and to understand them more. These are the 'illustrated notes' of what we saw. Of all listed buildings, those at Grades I and II*, or in Scotland Grades A and B, are in the top eight per cent. That most of the buildings in *Restoration* come from this top band illustrates how all-too-extensive the buildings at risk registers continue to be. One can hardly believe that places of the quality of, say, *Newstead Abbey* in Nottinghamshire (above) or *Strawberry Hill* in Middlesex (left) can still be at risk in this day and age. It is as if a sense of casual complacency has set in. This is dangerous indeed. Historic buildings remain deeply threatened, and it is a situation that could worsen if political pressures to 'modernise' the planning system in order to increase new housing development succeed in 'streamlining' (i.e. weakening) the systems of protection of historic buildings that were put in place after the planning disasters of the 1960s. Perhaps it is thought that people won't notice or no longer care. The success of the *Restoration* programme has been proof of the passion with which people do care.

Although the series was written off by some as 'elitist', it was clear from last year's programme that much affection remains for our abandoned country houses. To visit the *Archbishop's Palace* in Charing, near Ashford in Kent (previous page), is like returning to some parts of Normandy before the War. One enters through a ruinous gatehouse to find a beautiful and ancient medieval banqueting hall. But this has become a barn, with its delicate stone window tracery absorbed into later brickwork. Lean-to roofs and the inevitable corrugated iron prevail. And yet this is a scene that Edward II would remember. Indeed enough of the buildings survive to allow us to imagine that pre-Reformation world of ecclesiastical wealth and indulgence.

The *Hall of Clestrain* (this page), near Stromness on the island of Orkney, is also now a farm – indeed the building probably owes its survival to its most recent use as a pigsty. This symmetrical Palladian villa, alas now shorn of its central pediment and one of its pair of flanking outbuildings, still commands this section of bleak but magnificent coastline. In the mid-eighteenth century it must have been one of the most enlightened and exciting architectural ventures in the Northern Isles. You can still feel the radiating presence of this house from the long axial driveway and in the high proportions of the internal rooms. If you half close your eyes you could be in Tuscany. Can there ever have been a finer home for pigs?

A grey cemented façade and a dreary range of 1960s classrooms which seemingly
collide into the back of *Sherborne House* in Dorset (next page) immediately
suggest that it has endured a long period of institutional use. Inside, however,
lies a wonderful surprise. The entrance hall is designed so that each of its
internal walls is symmetrically composed, with a central section
brought forward with pilasters and a fully detailed entablature.
Not even the crude timber stanchions erected to support the old
school hall above can detract from this impressive joinery.
What one does not instantly appreciate is that this entrance
hall is merely an antechamber to the great painted staircase
by James Thornhill. This lies beyond the open door on
the left and should in itself warrant the immediate
preservation of this building.

A much older schoolroom survives, rather unexpectedly, in the Birmingham suburb of King's Norton (opposite). Here, in the *Old Grammar School*, the fake beams of the surrounding inter-war semis are upstaged by the real thing, all skilfully and robustly pegged together in English oak, with even the window tracery made of crisply carved timber. The arched wooden braces are cut to a curve like the Gothic ribs of a cathedral vault. This small school sent students to Oxbridge, and it is hard not to believe that such a beautiful room played an important role in their inspiration.

Less fortunate children in Cornwall found themselves mining for copper at a very early age down in the *South Caradon Mine* (this page). Although disused for over a century, these former pumping buildings still preside over the Cornish moorland with an eerie silence. They are the embodiment of ruins: giant, gaunt, windowless hulks, constructed of massive and skilfully bonded granite blocks. Clad in uncontrolled ivy, they rise up defiantly against the black stormy skies in memory of all those who endured the hardship of this place.

The fate of redundant police stations, courtrooms, and prisons has long been a challenge for those who seek to find new uses for these buildings without diluting the austerity of their character. *Armagh Gaol*, in Northern Ireland, developed in three major phases, but these always involved the extension rather than replacement of the existing buildings. Consequently this symmetrical late-Georgian entrance vestibule (left) determined the later axial placing of the Victorian ranges beyond. Whether the prisoners appreciated this sequence of handsomely proportioned doorways as they were unlocked may be doubtful, but good design is free and so there was nothing to lose. The use of classical architecture to convey a sense of order and discipline can also be seen in the no less frightening prospect of Llanfyllin Union Workhouse in Powys, Wales (below). Like a grim warning the building is separated from the town by a field, and one must have dreaded being sent there, with an often infinite sentence to serve.

Sheffield Manor Lodge served as the rather more comfortable prison for Mary, Queen of Scots. One encounters the ruins of this once venerable mansion quite suddenly in the midst of a typical modern council estate. A fine avenue of trees once led down the hill to the (then) small town of Sheffield and its castle. Now there are dual carriageways and a scattering of high-rise buildings, and an office block now stands on the site of the former castle. That such a venerable and significant piece of the city's history has survived the ravages of time is something of a miracle, and it should be treasured.

Although one would not think it at first glance, this Regency house (below) is *Cardigan Castle*, in the former county of Cardiganshire in Wales. It retains significant parts of its substantial and ancient military past, with high and massive retaining walls which contain the edge of the site, and a stout circular tower which subsequently became a very spooky kitchen. Initially it appears romantic in its decay – not even Hollywood could have produced the spectre of a house so overgrown and abandoned. But fifty years of neglect have taken their toll, as the vast gaping holes in its interior testify. Happily the authorities have at last taken the property into their possession, an illustration of the action that can be taken against those who refuse to look after the historic built environment. Whatever individual owners may say, these old buildings are the physical record of our past and culture, and ultimately the belong to us all.

RESTORATION

WALES

Cardigan Castle CARDIGAN

Llanfyllin Union Workhouse LLANFYLLIN

Celynen Workingmen's Institute NEWBRIDGE

Wales is joined to England but also cut off from it by ranges of mountains and hills. The history of Wales reflects this situation: for centuries, Wales has found relations with England difficult, but necessary. England's Roman rulers conquered Wales, but the Saxons did not. The Normans tried to, building many castles in the process. So the turbulent history of medieval Wales, with Welsh lords fighting their Norman–English counterparts, has left a huge imprint on the landscape, and castles such as Caernarfon, Conwy, and Harlech are still among Britain's most magnificent buildings.

The Welsh responded in kind and the oldest of the three restoration candidates in Wales is Cardigan Castle, which is one of the earliest substantial castles built by a Welsh lord. It has a remarkable history, occupied and extended in turn by the Welsh and English as the fortunes of the two sides ebbed and flowed through the twelfth and thirteenth centuries. It was finally put beyond military use by the Parliamentarian army during the Civil War, but its story did not end then. In contrast to so many medieval castles that survive as gaunt ruins unoccupied since Cromwell's time, Cardigan acquired elegant new buildings in the eighteenth century, and began a new history as a house.

Cardigan Castle has another claim to fame. It was host to the first Eisteddfod, and so played a part in the creation of one

Cardigan Castle across the River Teifi.

At the heart of Llanfyllin Union Workhouse, the three-storey Master's accommodation gives a good view of the entire complex.

of the icons of Welsh culture. There is something fitting in the fact that a building born out of conflict should be the site of a peaceful meeting at which culture could be celebrated in peaceful competition.

The castle was not the only type of building that could stand for oppression and gloom. In the nineteenth century, with no welfare state, there was one place above all that inspired dread for the poor: the workhouse. For those unfortunate people who had no work or support from others in their family, the local workhouse was the only refuge. It was designed to be uninviting, and represented a regime of Spartan conditions, poor food, and, above all, loss of dignity for the inmates. So disliked were the workhouses that most were either demolished or converted to other uses when the welfare state was established after World War II.

However, one, the Llanfyllin Union Workhouse, remains largely intact. For many, there is still a stigma attached to the building. But it is a part of Welsh history and is a substantial, usable building that deserves to be restored. Its advocates hope that finding a new use for the building will give it new meaning, just as the arrival of the Eisteddfod gave a new meaning to Cardigan Castle.

For the majority, Welsh culture was very different from the life either of castle or workhouse. By the mid-nineteenth century, the coalfields of South Wales were bringing huge wealth to the mine-owners and employment to millions – both in the mines and in the industries that sprang up around them. South Wales was booming, but at a cost. The work was hard and dangerous and the hours were long. Yet the Welsh clung to their culture and many miners longed for better leisure facilities and the opportunity for self-improvement.

One result of this longing was the creation of the miners' institutes, buildings that contained libraries and leisure facilities where the workmen and their families could relax, enjoy themselves, and even improve their education. The remaining Welsh restoration candidate is one of the most remarkable of these buildings, at Newbridge in South Wales. It shows how the tradition of culture and literacy represented by the Eisteddfod could also develop into something that could be enjoyed every week, in the miners' scarce hours away from the coal face.

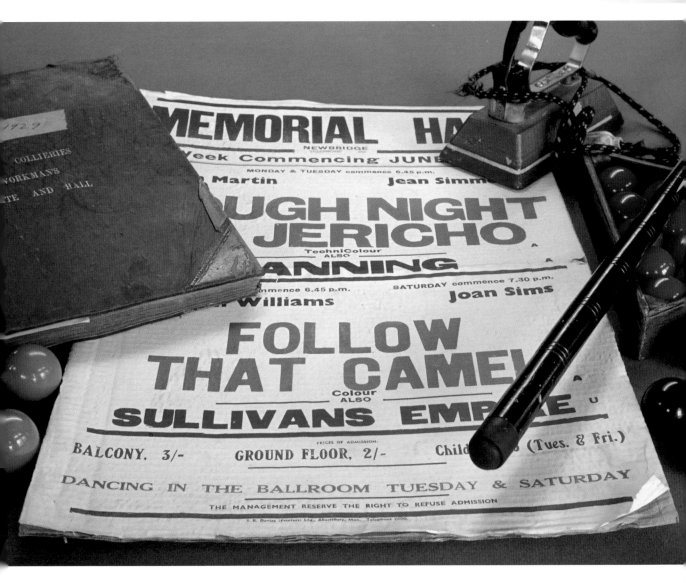

For much of the twentieth century, buildings like the Newbridge Miners' Institute – together with the adjacent Memorial Hall with its dance floor and cinema – were the focus of life for Welsh communities. They provided somewhere to go in an era when transport was difficult. But just as importantly, they offered uplift and inspiration to people whose main outlook was the four walls of a small miner's cottage and the dark and dangerous passages of the pit.

All three restoration candidates in Wales offer uplifting architecture and tell fascinating historical stories. They are outstanding examples of the Welsh contribution to our historic built environment.

Dancing, film-going, and snooker were three of the activities on offer at the Workingmen's Institute and Memorial Hall at Newbridge, the social centre for miners and their families.

Cardigan Castle

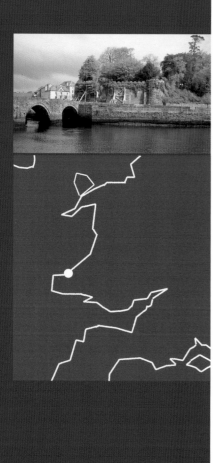

Wales is famous for its castles. For much of the Middle Ages the English and the Welsh contended for control of the country and its borders, and the castles built by English rulers such as Edward I are some of the finest ever constructed. But there are also less well-known castles, built by Welsh lords and rulers. One with an especially interesting history is in the town of Ceredigion, or Cardigan.

Glen Johnson, who works for the local authority in Cardigan and has been involved with plans for the castle for many years, explained that the site has been important for the town, but has also been a source of mystery: 'The site makes up a big chunk of the town centre, but for years it was in private hands and the public were denied entry. So it became a kind of secret garden for Cardigan. Many locals who had seen only photographs of the inside were surprised at the size of the buildings in the grounds.' Now the opportunity has come to restore the building and open it regularly.

Fortifications in the area go back almost to the Norman Conquest. A Norman lord, Roger of Montgomery, built a castle near Cardigan in 1093 as part of the conquerors' attempts to push their power west into Wales. This was probably a wood-and-earth castle about a mile to the west of the modern town centre. A few years later another Norman, Gilbert de Clare, founded the town and built another wooden castle to defend it. But the Welsh did not stand by. In around 1170 a local prince called Rhys ap Gruffydd – better known simply as Lord Rhys – attacked the town and took the new castle from its Norman occupiers. He soon set about rebuilding it, this time in stone.

This was a momentous project, said to be the first Welsh stone castle, and Rhys threw a huge banquet on Christmas Day in 1176 to celebrate the building's completion. Part of the celebration was a pair of competitions – one between poets, another featuring musicians – with a chair of honour and lavish prizes for the winner of each. Welsh lords had always held contests for bards and harpers, but this one, because of the scale of the event, stood out as something special. For many it marks the birth of the Eisteddfod, the uniquely Welsh cultural

All most people see of Cardigan Castle is the curtain wall (left), and this is barely visible behind layers of vegetation and strong steel supports.

Glen Johnson and castle supporter Sue Lewis (above) contemplate the state of the grounds in front of Castle Green House.

festival that still attracts thousands of visitors today. Glen Johnson explained that this heritage gives the castle a special importance for Welsh people: 'Because it hosted this iconic event the place has a particular significance in Wales.'

Rhys was influential in other ways, too. He became an ally of the English king, Henry II, realising that, if he could not beat the English, he could certainly gain their respect. And his skill as a warrior, diplomat, lawgiver, and man of culture made him the dominant Welsh prince of his time. He stood for political stability, but this did not last after his death in 1197. His two sons squabbled over their inheritance, eventually selling Cardigan Castle to the new English king, John, and the place repeatedly changed hands between Welsh and Normans for the next half century. By 1244 it was in the hands of the Norman lord Robert Waleran, who improved its fortifications – many of the remains visible on the ground today date from his time. The site remained important, becoming a major administrative centre under Edward I and an important possession of Henry VII, who presented it to Catherine of Aragon as a dowry when she was betrothed to his son, Prince Arthur. The castle stood proud and strong until the time of the Civil War, when it was attacked by the Parliamentarian army. After a struggle the castle fell and the roundheads slighted it, making sure that it was in such a ruinous state that it could no longer be occupied or used against them.

But Cromwell's men left enough to give us a hint of how strong the castle might have been. The site is still impressive, overlooking the river. This was important even in Norman times, when Cardigan quickly became a trading port. By the time Henry VII visited in 1485, it was one of the busiest ports in Wales.

Stretches of the castle's curtain wall remain, scarred by the Parliamentarians and affected by more recent buildings, but still there. They date mostly from the time of Waleran, but archaeological investigation in 1990 revealed that some at least stand on earlier foundations – presumably those of the stone castle completed by Rhys in 1176. In addition, several stretches of medieval wall snake through the later developments in Cardigan itself, for Waleran fortified the town as well as the castle. These walls contain local stone, but records from the mid-thirteenth century reveal that a great deal of stone was also ordered from Gloucestershire, so there may be Cotswold stone here among Cardigan's fortifications.

An ornate fanlight (below) hints at the Regency glory of Castle Green House.

There are also the remains of some of the castle's towers, again dating from Waleran's time. Round in shape, these are lower than they would have been originally, and in some places the narrow arrow loops have been replaced by later windows. But their thick walls remain to give an idea of

Banded masonry (right) is a striking feature of the walls of the house.

the strength of Waleran's work – they were not going to fall easily, even to Cromwell's powerful bombardment.

One look at the site shows that the castle had a second, much later heyday. By the beginning of the nineteenth century, when all that stood were a couple of towers and a wall, a local barrister called John Bowen bought the ruins. In 1808 he built

himself a new house on the site of the castle keep, using part of the old structure including the vaulted basement, which became his cellar. Bowen's previous house had been designed by John Nash, the celebrated Regency architect who designed a number of houses in Wales before beginning his more famous work in London for the Prince Regent. So Bowen included a number of fashionable Regency elements in his new design, Castle Green House – a grand Gothic-style window on

Plants inhabiting the guttering and peeling render suggest that the house is a victim of the elements – especially damp.

Much of the interior woodwork has been removed and the decorations are peeling. An abandoned doll's house seems to mirror the state of the full-size building.

the stairs, for example. Another unusual feature is provided by the round windows at the front of the house – only one other building in the town, Imperial House, has such windows and this was built a few years after Castle Green and was probably copied from Bowen's building.

Castle Green House also has elements that are typical of the local building style. One such is the banded stonework, typical of the Cardigan and St Dogmael's area. This style of masonry is said to have been brought over to Britain by French monks,

who in turn copied it from the Byzantine buildings of
Constantinople, where it is still visible on the massive city walls.
This medieval military influence seems fitting in a house that
incorporates the tower of a thirteenth-century castle in its
structure. Like so many British buildings, Castle Green House is
a hybrid, and no less fascinating for that.

Inside, too, there are traces of the long history of the house. A
barrel-vaulted cellar survives, as do eight-foot-thick walls in the
kitchen, both taken over from the medieval castle fabric. There

Painting trellis is hard
and fiddly work. This one
seems not to have been
painted since it was
installed in the
nineteenth century.

are some moulded ceilings and wooden panelling from the Regency period. Later generations have also added touches, such as some early twentieth-century hand-painted wallpaper in one of the bedrooms.

The property has been in private hands until very recently, meaning that it has been one of the 'lost' castles of Wales, visible from the outside but with interiors known only to a select few. But now the castle has been bought by the local council the prospects are good for making the building more accessible. There have already been a number of successful public open days.

One of the benefits of restoration would be to allow the public to visit the site, and there is strong local support for the campaign to save the castle. The Ceredigion council, for whom

A nineteenth-century fire surround is coming apart and the grate is partly concealed by a later stove. But the components are there and the fireplace could be restored to form, once again, the focal point of the room.

this is a large project, together with local supporters, are forming a Building Preservation Trust. Plans are at an early stage but there are plenty of ideas about how the building could be used. One popular idea is to use the house as a national exhibition centre for the Eisteddfod movement. A town heritage centre, a museum of Welsh genealogy, and craft workshops are other possibilities. A mix of uses will probably be the result, including both exhibition space and commercial functions. But, as Glen Johnson stressed, the aim will be to allow commercial uses that fit in with the age of the building and its role as a visitor attraction. With the locals, the council, and the Welsh Assembly behind the scheme, it seems likely that the public will once more be able to have access to a site with a very special place in the history of Wales.

Pointed Gothic Revival windows hark back to the Regency heyday of Castle Green House – and seem fitting in the context of the medieval castle that surrounds it.

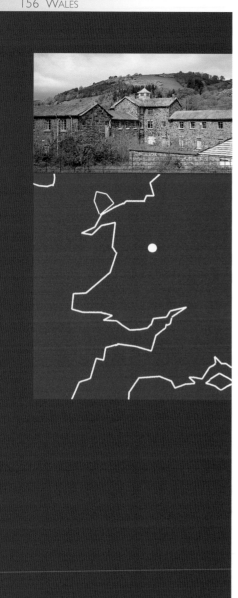

Llanfyllin Union Workhouse

We often look at the buildings of the past with nostalgia, or value them for what they tell us about lifestyles more privileged than our own. High-status paintings or carvings on the walls are often just as important as the fabric of the building itself. But some buildings serve as reminders of the bad times – of crime or illness or poverty. One such building type is the workhouse, where the poor of the Victorian period and the early twentieth century were housed, often in conditions renowned for their harshness. Such buildings are just as much a part of our history as the country houses of the rich.

One of the few early workhouses to survive complete is the Union Workhouse, on the outskirts of Llanfyllin, in Powys. Hilary Collins, a local resident who bought the workhouse in order to save it, explained its importance: 'It is a building with a huge social significance for the local area, serving the poor for decades and then becoming a successful old people's home. It is also notable architecturally, and is the work of Thomas Penson, who was part of a dynasty of local surveyors and architects. Finally, the building has a wider importance, because there are now very few workhouses left that retain as much of the original fabric.'

The Llanfyllin workhouse is an uncompromising monument to a long-vanished system that grew out of specific needs in the 1830s. In the early nineteenth century the impoverished were helped by a system of 'poor relief', funded by a tax paid by local people. Many poor received 'outdoor relief', which enabled them to stay in their own homes. But the rich objected to the cost of this and, in 1834, Parliament passed the Poor Law Amendment Act.

The new act curtailed outdoor relief, making help available mainly through a network of workhouses. Parishes were grouped into Poor Law Unions, each of which was led by a Board of Guardians who ran the local workhouse. Anyone who wanted to be admitted to a workhouse had to pass a strict test, designed to exclude all but the most needy. Edwin Chadwick, the lawyer, writer, and reformer who devised the scheme, expressed clearly enough what he was about. Workhouses were meant to offer an environment that deterred all but genuine cases from wanting admission. As he put it, they should be 'uninviting places of wholesome restraint'.

The workhouse at Llanfyllin was built in 1838, four years after the passing of the Poor Law Amendment Act. There was certainly a need for poor relief locally. New technology was taking jobs away from the many farm workers and there was a slump in the textile industry following the end of the Napoleonic Wars. As a result of factors like these, unemployment was high and the gap between rich and poor was widening. So the Board of Guardians, drawn from the two dozen parishes of the local Poor Law Union, authorised a large workhouse, with room enough for two hundred and fifty inmates. They set a budget and commissioned the county surveyor, Thomas Penson, to design the building.

Penson based his building on a standard workhouse layout produced by Sampson Kempthorne, architect to the Poor Law Commissioners. Kempthorne's layout drew on the principle, devised by the reformer Jeremy Bentham, of the 'Panopticon' (the name comes from a Greek word meaning 'all-seeing') in

With their rubble walls and brick window surrounds, most of the buildings at the workhouse have no pretensions to grandeur, just a rather forbidding solidity.

which cells or wings radiate from a central supervisory hub. At Llanfyllin, the tall central building, where the Master lived, gave clear views of four wings, which radiated from it like the arms of a cross. This entire arrangement was surrounded by further wings, so that a plan or aerial view of the complex looks like a cross contained inside a square.

This was a highly practical plan. It provided distinct wings for men, women, and children, who were forced to live separately once they entered the workhouse. There was also a wing for kitchens, stores, and the dining area (inmates dined together, but the sexes sat separately). Other buildings contained such facilities as a bakery and laundry. The spaces between the wings were used as segregated exercise yards for the men, women, and children, with a fourth yard used as the Master's garden.

The entire structure has an uncompromising, forbidding aspect. It is built of stone – mostly local stone, to keep the cost down – with slate roofs. The windows are iron-framed, with only small opening sections. Such windows were often specified for workhouses, lunatic asylums, and schools, because they prevented children falling out or inmates escaping. The north-western façade, that which faces Llanfyllin, is slightly less forbidding than the others. Here Penson allowed himself the luxury of classical details, such as Venetian windows (three-part windows in which the central section has a rounded top and is taller than the flanking ones). This façade has other details, such as dressings in lighter stone, which give it a 'higher-status' appearance. The aim must have been to improve the view from the town, but the architect may also have wanted to give the building a less prison-like image, because there had been considerable unrest in Wales when the new system of poor relief was introduced. Overall, though, there is no mistaking what the building is for – it radiates feelings of uniformity, solidity, and restraint.

Supporter and trustee Wynne Morris looks at the buildings of the workhouse.

Inside, it would have been a similar story, although the interior has been much altered and stripped of most of its original fittings. But the old staircases, plain and solid, remain, and some rooms still have limewash on the walls. Other telling details can also be seen, from meat hooks in the cellar beneath the kitchen to the remains of fireplaces – the workhouse was heated with the cheapest available coal.

The treatment the inmates received was as austere as the building. On arrival, men and women were interviewed and if granted admission were separated, given a medical examination, bathed, and issued with their workhouse uniform of coarse cloth. Any possessions were taken from them and put into storage and from then on it was a daily routine of ten hours' work and a diet dominated by gruel, bread, and potatoes. Women did cleaning or kitchen work while the men tended the workhouse gardens and looked after the pigs, helping to keep the institution as self-sufficient as possible.

The simple stairs and plain plasterwork survive – just – to give an impression of the Spartan conditions endured by the original inmates.

Good conduct was expected at all times and bad behaviour was punished, sometimes with twenty-four hours' solitary confinement and a still more basic diet. Children, too, were expected to be on their best behaviour. They were taught reading, writing, arithmetic, religious studies, and useful skills, but by the age of eight or nine they were expected to work – the boys with local tradesmen and the girls in domestic service. In theory, living in the workhouse was voluntary, but in practice there was little alternative for many inmates and they often felt imprisoned. And there was a stigma attached to the place that still lingers.

For the history of the workhouse lasted well into the twentieth century. The strictures of the Poor Law Amendment Act continued until it was repealed in 1930. By this time, the regime at the workhouse was probably more humane than it had been almost a century before, but life there was still harsh. After 1930, it continued to look after the inmates who could not leave, most of whom were elderly or ill. Eventually the place became an old people's home, continuing in this role until it finally closed in 1982.

In the late 1980s the building was converted to an outdoor activities centre, but this business went into receivership after one of the owners was killed when he fell off the roof. At this

Many of the internal partition walls have been removed and the graffiti artists have been at work. One challenge is to decide exactly which interior features to replace.

point, many of the interior fixtures and fittings were removed and the building was sold to developers, who left it unmaintained. Finally Hilary Collins bought the property in the hope of saving it. The process of transferring ownership to a Building Preservation Trust is under way, and the Trust has taken on board her proposals for a new use for the building.

The changes in the way the building was used meant that various alterations were made to the interiors of the workhouse. The dormitory accommodation was subdivided, although most of the partition walls have since been removed. Many of the chimney stacks were removed and some of the windows were replaced – many with steel-framed windows in the 1950s. For the architect Michael Goulden, this represents a challenge. He explained that many decisions have to be made about what to replace – in this case he favours reinstating the chimney stacks and the old-style windows. He is also keen to include information in the building about how it was altered over the years. The restored building will also look to the future, since energy-efficient systems, including biomass heating and solar water heating, are among the proposals.

The beautiful setting, against a backdrop of hills, is the result of the decision to build the workhouse on the edge of the town.

The hope is to use a substantial part of the building to house a crafts and antiques centre, with a large number of display units for regional craft workers and antique dealers. In addition there will be a number of visitor facilities, including a museum of local history featuring the workhouse system, a tourist information centre, a hall for community and trade events, a restaurant, and gardens. As Hilary Collins insisted, the aim is to create income to make the building sustainable: 'There is huge potential in this building. With perhaps one hundred and fifty different units selling antiques, the workhouse would attract visitors from far and wide, bringing great economic benefit to a town that has been hit badly by the downturn after the epidemic of foot and mouth disease. With the potential for a local museum or heritage centre, together with gardens and a restaurant, there would be something for everyone. It is the potential variety of things happening on one site that makes it so attractive.' The scheme is challenging – not least because the repressive history of the building is still a negative factor for many locals. But the hope is that restoration will encourage regeneration for the Llanfyllin area, and that the benefits that this will bring will show the old workhouse in a positive new light.

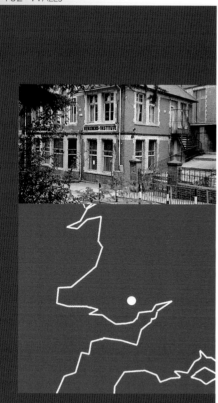

Celynen Workingmen's Institute and Memorial Hall

For millions in the valleys of South Wales, coal mining was a way of life for much of the twentieth century. Countless British factories and power stations, not to mention domestic hearths, relied on coal from South Wales. And that meant relying on Welsh miners, who did the exhausting and dangerous work of extracting the coal. When their shift was over, Welsh miners had little money for leisure and little time to travel beyond their town or village. At the turn of the century the local pub was the most likely place to find a miner on his day off. But, in 1898, a group of miners at the Celynen Colliery in Newbridge decided they deserved something better.

The miners formed a committee with the aim of improving the social facilities available to working people in their town. They met at a coffee house owned by the colliery company and were allowed to use a room there rent-free. The welfare scheme proved popular but soon the miners decided that they

needed something more – better premises and more facilities than could be provided at the local coffee house. They decided to build new premises. As local man Howard Stone emphasised, this was a remarkable decision: 'It was incredibly courageous of the miners to take on a project like this. It was unheard-of for a miner to take out a mortgage in the early 1900s, but because of their bravery, the Newbridge miners got a state-of-the-art building for the community.'

The vision was to create a multi-purpose building that would provide an alternative to the pub. Originally there was no licence to sell alcohol – the idea was to cater for the wives and children as well as the miners themselves, to create a place where whole families, and the whole community, could come together to relax and enjoy games such as snooker. The founders had educational aspirations, too – there would be a reading room with books and newspapers, to give the users some intellectual stimulation.

It was an ambitious scheme and the committee had very little money. But they found a site belonging to the local council, bought it from them at a very favourable price, and took out a mortgage to pay for a building and its fixtures and fittings. Their building was opened in August 1908, and it served the local miners and their families well. They were blazing a trail. By the time they had paid off the mortgage in 1922, a miners' welfare fund had been established by the government to provide facilities such as institutes and pithead baths. The miners of Celynen were more than ten years ahead of their time.

At the time the institute was built, the miners of Celynen could afford to be optimistic. Their pit was a sizeable one. At the turn of the century it employed over 1,700 men to produce around 10,000 tons of coal per week. They were proud of their hard work and productivity and they put up a building that was worthy of their pride.

Local red brick was used for the walls, set off with dressings of yellow brick and tile-work. The roofs were of Welsh slate. The tall, imposing gables and big windows made a powerful

Supporters Andrew Gadd (left) and Howard Stone stand next to the fine brickwork of a window surround.

The institute (opposite) stands close to the street and the tall memorial hall is set further back. Neither building has a striking exterior and their brickwork is in keeping with the style of the street. They save their glories for inside.

statement in a landscape of pithead gear and small miners' houses. Inside, it was even more impressive. There was a hall with four snooker tables on the right-hand side and on the left a long reading room with tables on which the newspapers were laid out. Upstairs was the library, a large room partly oak panelled and partly lined with bookshelves, staffed by a full-time librarian and a part-time assistant. There was also a committee room, which was used as a lodge by the local branch of the union. These facilities had the overwhelming support of the local miners – records show that in the institute's first year it had 1,580 members.

It was, and is, a fine building, though not as big as some of the later miners' institutes, built for the larger collieries with the support of the Miners' Welfare Committee. These subsidised institutes could have four or five floors and some of them even had a swimming pool. But the Newbridge building is more remarkable because it was built by the miners themselves, and sprang from their aspirations for better social conditions and education through self-help.

The cinema interior is a kaleidoscope of coloured glass, gilding, and mouldings. It transported its audiences into another world.

By the early 1920s these aspirations went still further. It was decided to build a hall with dance floor, cinema, and theatre. In the era before television, these were the three most popular forms of entertainment. Newbridge already had a cinema, called the Grand, but it was not unusual for small towns to have two 'picture houses' in this period and, when cars were the preserve of the rich, there was plenty of demand for inexpensive entertainment close to home. The new building was to be a memorial hall, built in memory of the miners who had lost their lives in World War I, so, as Howard Stone pointed out, 'The idea of the bravery of the miners was once again to the fore.' The new hall was sited next to the institute although it was physically separate from it – a connecting building was added later.

The memorial hall is built in a similar style to the institute, in red brick with dressings of yellow brick and Bath stone. As with the earlier building, the real surprises are inside, this time with a decorative scheme designed to take the colliers and their

The interior decoration uses an eclectic mix of motifs. Many of the details, such as the mouldings and keystones, are classical, but they are combined in a way that conjures up the spirit of the 1920s.

families into another, visually richer world. Miraculously, much of this decoration still survives. Downstairs was the dance hall with its superb sprung floor – kept highly polished and said to be one of the best in the area. Today the space has a modern suspended ceiling, but above this the original plasterwork, with its central rosette, survives.

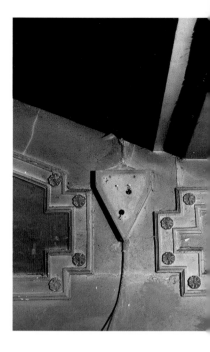

Above is the cinema, a space which is designed to double as a theatre. When showing visitors around the memorial hall, Howard Stone often pauses outside the entrance to the cinema saying, 'Wait to be amazed' – and the effect is truly amazing. The auditorium is decorated in a way that shows the influence of the art deco style, which was just becoming fashionable. In typical art deco fashion, it draws on many influences – there were pierced screens in the Islamic manner and more uncompromisingly modern art deco light fittings. Many of these details are preserved – not all in situ, but kept safe elsewhere in the building, ready for restoration. Screens, light fittings, and the ground-floor box office are all retained for reinstatement. The seats on the lower level have been removed but many of these are also kept upstairs. Some decorative details, such as the wall paintings of mining scenes, are still in place. Still others, such as the murals of scouting scenes, have been added more recently.

The use of the space for live theatre has also left behind some fascinating details. The original art deco stage curtains are still in place, with their bands of blue and gold. And behind the proscenium arch is the network of ropes that controlled both these curtains and the scenery. The whole space is astonishing, its remarkable decoration lifting the spirits in a way that few other buildings in the area could manage.

It is not hard to imagine the backstage area thronging with actors and technicians and the auditorium full of local families, eagerly awaiting the next performance from an amateur

The interior of the institute is plainer than that of the memorial hall, with painted panelling and simple wooden furniture.

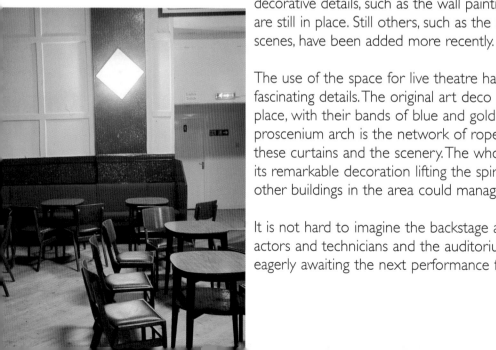

company or a professional touring group. Drama festivals and competitions were so popular here that you often had to queue for hours for tickets.

With both films and live theatre possible, the memorial hall provided a variety of fare. There were two different cinema programmes per week, each featuring a 'big picture', a short film, a newsreel, and a cartoon. Add the live performances in the theatre and a night at the dance hall, and locals had as good a choice of entertainment as they could expect. And all

From the panelled walls to the windows with their heart-shaped pattern, from the ceiling rose to the original art deco curtain, a selection of details shows the quality of the cinema auditorium.

Original projection equipment waits to be reinstalled.

From Bogart to Sinatra, the cinema offered a variety of Hollywood entertainment that was as glamorous as its own shimmering interior.

this was in addition to the Welsh propensity for music-making that found fulfilment in local choirs and in the silver band, which rehearsed regularly in the institute. The miner's life was hard, but he could play hard too.

But soon a shadow was passing over the colliery. In the inter-war years a series of fatal accidents gave the mine a bad reputation, earning it the nickname 'the blood tub'. But the miners, the owners, and the Coal Board, which took over when the mines were nationalised in 1947, knew that mining was a risky business. The pit continued, using its steam-powered engine to raise the coal until it was electrified in 1971. The last miners clocked off in 1985, leaving the institute and memorial hall as monuments to their enterprise in working to improve their lot.

Following the closure of the mine the memorial hall spent a time as a rather lacklustre workingmen's club, which then closed, leaving behind little except debts and memories of the hall in its earlier, better, days. But local supporters have rallied, got the building listed, and put on successful fund-raising events. Howard Stone's wish is to see the memorial hall and institute restored so that they can play the central part in community life that they did in their heyday: 'I want my grandchildren, and their children, to see the beauty that I saw and enjoy the benefit that I had.' Then the huge potential of these special buildings will be realised once again.

RESTORATION Update Wales
News from the first series

Since Llanelly House appeared on *Restoration*, there has been a huge increase in public interest and support for the building, especially in the town itself and in Wales, but also across the United Kingdom. On site, investigative work and detailed paint analysis have been under way, ready for the preparation of a detailed conservation plan. The ultimate goal is to conserve the house and make it available for two kinds of use: on the one hand, interpretation of the building's history and displays that the public can access, together with visitor facilities such as a restaurant; on the other, accommodation for officers serving the arts and community functions of the local authority or other related agency.

There have been major developments at Vaynol Old Hall and the conservation school that is based at Vaynol. A major grant of European Objective 1 funding has been made and there are further grant applications in the pipeline, including one for re-roofing the hall. The school is also benefiting from a link with an established heritage contractor, providing work for students when they finish their courses.

RESTORATION

SCOTLAND

Portencross Castle WEST KILBRIDE

Hall of Clestrain ORKNEY

Knockando Wool Mill MORAYSHIRE

Scotland is a large and varied part of the United Kingdom. In the 250 miles or so from the borders to the far north are the rich lowland farmland, the cities known both for their elegance and their industry, and the ancient mountains of the Highlands. Rivers and lochs of great beauty punctuate this landscape, and beyond the sea are Orkney and Shetland to the north, and the countless Western Isles – all separate, and staunchly independent, communities.

The cities of the central lowlands, especially Glasgow and Edinburgh, are major centres of population. But apart from places such as these, Scotland is for the most part very sparsely populated – the landscape can be breathtakingly empty. For centuries much of the country's economy has been rural. People have made their living farming and processing the products of farming. Two of Scotland's most famous industries – the manufacture of textiles and the production of whisky – rely on wool and barley grown locally and on the power and the very taste of the local water.

Scotland's rural buildings are rooted in the land. In the Highlands, many are constructed of the local granite and slate, materials that were also brought south to make solid and long-lasting buildings. In the lowlands there are also red and grey sandstones. So there are plenty of materials to supply a rich architectural tradition that has flourished distinctively and independently from England.

And sometimes as a direct result of this independence. Portencross Castle, the oldest of the three Scottish candidates for restoration, is typical of the many tower houses that were built to protect the interests of Scotland's kings and lairds. Strongly built of stone and commanding an impressive position, it is as magnificent in its modern ruin as it must have been when it was new.

Towers like Portencross are at the roots of Scottish domestic architecture. Most started as simple stone towers, acquiring extensions as the need grew for extra space. Then, as the need for military protection became less pressing, some tower houses were turned into country houses, extra wings and comfortable apartments overwhelming the original building. Many is the mansion that can trace its beginnings to a spartan medieval tower. But Portencross did not grow in this way. Its main extension was added in the fourteenth century and it retains the proportions of a medieval tower house, a special survivor of the times when defence and protection were the most important things for a community living on the Scottish coast.

By the time the second of the three Scottish buildings was constructed, priorities had changed. The Hall of Clestrain is a

Portencross Castle overlooks a stretch of the Scottish west coast. As was the case with the other Scottish restoration candidates, a Speyside mill and a house on Orkney, water was crucial to its position and to the lives of its first users.

Georgian house by the sea on Orkney. Dating from the second half of the eighteenth century, it comes from a time when Scotland was experiencing a cultural renaissance. Edinburgh was expanding with the building of the squares and terraces of its New Town. Writers such as David Hulme were enhancing the reputation of Scottish philosophy, while painters like Sir Henry Raeburn were portraying the great and the good.

This whole movement, with its enthusiasm for classical architecture, was centred firmly on the capital. But buildings like the Hall of Clestrain show that it spread quickly as far as Orkney. It is a grand house, but it is not one of those eighteenth-century houses that has been imposed like an alien structure in the landscape. The Hall relies on its setting for its existence – like Portencross, it is inextricably linked to the nearby water, and a number of related structures such as a sail-store remind us that the sea was essential to the survival of the people of the island, not least the laird himself.

Isolated at the end of its drive, the Hall of Clestrain was designed to stand out in its quiet island setting. The lie of the land makes the adjoining garden walls virtually invisible.

The third Scottish restoration candidate also dates from the late eighteenth century and also began with a reliance on water. The Knockando Wool Mill used the flow of the local stream to power machinery for spinning yarn and weaving cloth made from the wool of the sheep that grazed the nearby fields. The whole enterprise was a potent coming together of the latest technology – the machines that drove the industrial revolution – with the available resources, wool and water power. Few buildings could be more grounded in their landscape, and it is a tribute to the building and its owner that it is still producing cloth today, although water power has been replaced by electricity.

All three Scottish candidates, then, are inseparable from their settings, and serve as tributes to local builders and local ways of life. They all deserve their local support and the support of all who are interested in the interaction between people, places, and buildings.

Tools and equipment catch light from the window at Knockando Wool Mill.

Portencross Castle

The site is stunning. Set on the west coast of Scotland near West Kilbride, Portencross Castle looks across the water towards the island of Little Cumbrae. The larger Isle of Bute lies beyond. This tall tower in its coastal setting looks every inch the archetypal Scottish tower house. But Portencross has historical importance too, because it was a favourite castle of Robert II, grandson of Robert Bruce and founder of the Stuart dynasty.

Before he was king, Robert held lands in Ayrshire, including the Isle of Bute with its castle of Rothesay. On the death of David II in 1371, Robert became king and it is thought that he stayed at Portencross on his journey from Rothesay to his coronation at Scone. He certainly used the castle often. Twelve of his royal charters, many of which kept in check the lords of the nearby isles, were issued from here and Portencross was a frequent stopping-off point on journeys to and from the royal estate on the island of Cumbrae.

According to tradition, the royal connection may go back much further. It is said that Portencross harbour was the embarkation point for many early Scottish kings when they made their final journey to their burial place on the island of Iona. Between 685 and 1058, some eighteen Scottish kings were buried on the island. This was long before the castle was built, but it points to a possible long-standing link between the kings of Scotland and this evocative location.

Like so many castles, Portencross was designed to make good use of its site. The tower enjoys a superb view of the harbour, so was ideally placed to keep a watch on passing shipping and near enough to the water for its occupants to set sail quickly if the need arose. This was important in the era before cannon, when the castle's occupants kept a sleek, fast boat, called a birlinn, rather like a Viking ship in appearance. This craft was quickly launched whenever it was necessary to intercept suspicious shipping in the Firth of Clyde. Another advantage of the site is that the tower is built on a rocky outcrop. The rocks provide a strong foundation for the massive stone walls.

But the castle was not always so large. Portencross started life in the mid-fourteenth century as a compact hall house,

Stone gables (left) remain to show the line of the original roof that sheltered the massive walls of Portencross Castle.

Alastair Glen, of the Friends of Portencross Castle, assesses the building's unique site.

perhaps a miniature version of the very large house built by Robert II at Dundonald, also in Ayrshire. In the late fourteenth or early fifteenth century, Portencross was extended. By this time the tower had acquired a wing containing extra accommodation, giving it the L-shaped plan of many Scottish tower houses. But Alastair Glen, chairman of the Friends of Portencross Castle, pointed out that here the plan is rather unusual. The extension was built on to the narrow end of the original tower, rather than on the long side as was more usual. The builders were probably influenced in this by the shape of the platform of rock on which the castle stands.

Around the tower there was probably a curtain wall, or barmkin, to give an added layer of security. If an enemy approached, this offered the local people some protection. At a sign of danger, the watchman would ring a bell and the community could gather behind the sheltering wall. Although it is not known for sure if Portencross had such an enclosure in the Middle Ages, a document of 1621 refers to a barn and barnyard on the site, and these may have been within an earlier curtain wall.

In other ways, the exterior is typical of Scottish tower houses. The masonry is mostly red sandstone, which was quarried on site and used for the main parts of all the walls. The corners are built with large blocks of white stone, their enormous mass adding strength to the parts of the building that are weakest under attack. Although now worn away, render, known in Scotland as harling, originally covered the walls. This smoothed over any unevennesses in the stone, but it also had a more practical purpose. Like the lime mortar between the stones, the harling allowed the stone to breathe while giving the building's exterior a waterproof 'skin'.

The castle's walls (above) are set firmly on foundations of natural rock. Large rectangular corner stones give the building added strength.

The loss of the harling is not the only change the building has seen. To begin with, the castle would have had only tiny windows, to keep out attackers and their arrows. With glass an expensive luxury during the Middle Ages, it is likely that only the upper half of each opening would have been glazed while a wooden shutter would have covered the lower section. In the seventeenth century, comfort and convenience became higher priorities and the castle's owners installed larger windows on the upper storeys.

The castle is built of red sandstone (right) that actually displays a rich palette of reds, greens, and greys.

Although the main structure has nearly all survived, the castle's roof came off in a storm in

1739. There is a flat concrete roof, which was put on in 1910 to keep the structure watertight. But this addition is deteriorating and has become a habitat for grass, shrubs, and other plant life. The roof's iron reinforcements are rusting and lime is leaching out of the concrete and forming impressive stalactites below. So this roofing structure, which has protected the building for nearly a century, is now a threat. If it collapsed it could bring down some of the ancient fabric with it.

If this happened, the castle's interiors could be badly affected. And these interiors are perhaps even more impressive than the exterior. Today, one enters the building through a ground-level doorway that leads to the lower floor of the castle. This room, with its vaulted ceiling, is impressive. Below ground level lies a bottle-shaped dungeon that was large enough to hold three or four prisoners. This structure is full of rubble now. As Alastair Glen pointed out, a former dungeon is not much use if it is not required for its original function. So, like many other similar structures, it was filled in.

Originally, the castle would have had a second entrance, with an exterior staircase, which would have given access to the first-floor hall, the main room of the castle. Both the lower room and the hall are barrel-vaulted, their impressive, tunnel-like ceilings indicating that this is a high-status building.

The hall has changed in appearance during its 600-year history. It would have been brightly painted, there would have been gilt stone carvings, and wall hangings may have given extra comfort, especially when a royal visitor arrived. There would have been a roaring fire, too, and although the present fireplace was added in the seventeenth century, there is evidence in the masonry of the line of the fourteenth-century original. The barrel vault and a well-made stone window seat remain as evidence of the room's status.

Barrel vaults were difficult and time-consuming to build. First of all, a wooden structure called centring was built in the shape of the underside of the vault, with basketwork used to get the curving shape exactly right. Once the centring was in position in the room, the masons started work fitting the stones above. They began at the sides, working towards the middle until they slotted the centre stones in position and all the stonework

An elevated platform gave the camera crew of *Restoration* a superb view of the building and its coastal setting.

The remains of a stone window seat hint that the castle offered a degree of comfort – it was not merely a building for military use but also played host to visiting royalty.

An iron-studded door has played three roles – keeping out enemies, repelling trespassers, and now simply waiting to be rehung.

'locked' in place. Next they mixed mortar and poured it over the top of the stonework, and when this had set they removed the centring, although they sometimes left the basketwork layer, covering it with a finishing coat of plaster.

There is a massive weight of stone in a barrel-vaulted ceiling like this, and this, together with the two-metre-thick walls, gives the castle immense strength. But over the years much of the mortar has worn away, and now the pressure of stone against stone is the main thing holding up the ceiling. If one of the centre stones was dislodged, the rest of the stones in the vault would be 'unlocked' and the whole ceiling would be at risk. Then this great weight of stone, for so long a strength, would become a liability.

The Friends of Portencross Castle have been working since 1998 to make the case for the building's restoration. Although there has already been a feasibility study supported by archaeological and other reports, the Friends are keen to point out that before any work can start, a full archaeological study will be undertaken. Archaeologists will be examining the floors and walls with great care, both recording what is there and working out how the castle looked at different stages in its history. Once this is done, the physical work of restoration can begin. The plans are to consolidate the structure and give the castle a new roof in the style of the original. The barrel vaults will be repaired by pouring mortar from above, just as the medieval builders would have done. And the floors throughout the building will be improved. Information and displays about the castle's history will be installed.

But perhaps the greatest challenge will be the work needed on the castle's foundations. Currently the waves are undercutting the rock on which the building stands and eventually, if left untreated, the stone will slide into the water, taking the castle with it. The plan is to anchor the structure with concrete and stainless steel rods drilled deep into the bedrock.

This is a challenging scheme, but it has plenty of backing. Alastair Glen recalled that the movement to save the castle gathered strength when the building was put up for sale. 'There was overwhelming local support to retain the castle, and the nearby stretch of foreshore, in public ownership. We asked people to sign a petition,' he remembered. 'In a few months we had gathered four thousand signatures. Everyone supports what we're doing.' It is an impressive response for a small group based in a thinly populated rural area. And this enthusiasm is reflected by visitors to the area. A survey found that 91 per cent of visitors wanted to see the interior of the castle.

All this enthusiasm has already had practical results. As well as garnering political support, the Friends have been raising money, including a maximum grant from the Architectural Heritage Fund for a feasibility study. As a result, the Friends now have clear plans for restoration, backed up with technical studies covering issues such as structure and archaeology. The movement to restore Portencross Castle is well on its way.

The dark interior seems to cry out for the light of flaming torches.

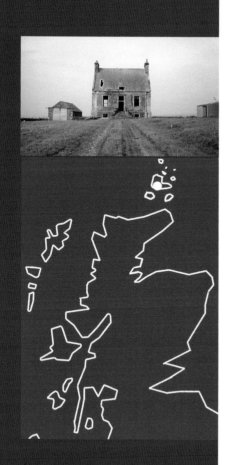

Hall of Clestrain

Nowhere in Orkney is far from the sea. The Hall of Clestrain – the name describes both the big house and the local district – is nearer than most, and its site reminds the visitor that life on Orkney in the past depended on the sea, and that fishing was almost as important a source of food as farming. Steve Callaghan of Historic Scotland, who has been closely involved with the plans for the Hall and its surroundings, described the view. 'As you approach the site from the main road, the scenery is magical. Apart from the Hall itself, the view is all things sea. We are near Stromness Harbour and the big new ferry passes nearby. The high cliffs of the island of Hoy are visible, and so are two lighthouses and the buoys that guide the boats in the sailing regatta. Down by the shore, the beautiful natural harbour has been modified by local builders and boatmen. There is a near-perfect 'noust', where boats were stored, and an old storage building was a haunt of smugglers.'

In the middle of all this is the Hall of Clestrain itself, a Georgian laird's house that was built in 1769. It is a substantial house but it is not huge – on the main floor there is just one window either side of the front door. And it is in a bad way – the original roof has gone, many of the windows are bricked up, and a rough stone wall has replaced the original iron balustrade that once framed the steps up to the entrance. But even in its current state, there are enough hints of its original grandeur to make it an obvious restoration candidate.

From the front, it is rather like a Georgian doll's house. The broad stone steps leading to the front door, the large windows to the main floor, and the dressed-stone window surrounds, all show that the original owners wanted to create a sense of grandeur. From the side, one can see that the house is built to a square plan. This is quite unusual, as such houses were usually rectangular, but the overall effect of the design, with the sash windows and balanced proportions, is still unmistakably Georgian.

The style of the house is radically different from the usual houses of Orkney. In the eighteenth century most islanders lived in low, stone-walled, thatch-roofed houses. They shared their homes with livestock and poultry, slept on straw or heather mattresses, and kept warm by huddling around a central fire. There were no windows and the smoke from the fire escaped through a hole in the roof. The laird's house, with its glazed windows, fireplaces, and elegant decoration, was a world away in both comfort and sophistication. Indeed a house like this would not look out of place in Edinburgh, and at least one building of very similar design has been found there.

It was not uncommon in the eighteenth century for lairds on Orkney to look south for their architectural inspiration. In former times, Orkney did not seem as isolated as it does now. This is because it was on a major shipping route. Many vessels, bound

The site of the Hall of Clestrain is visible in the distance across Clestrain Sound to Hoy and Stromness.

The door, windows, original roof covering, and entrance-stair banisters have all gone from the once-grand entrance front.

across the Atlantic, started their voyage by sailing up Britain's east coast, stopping at Orkney for water and provisions before beginning the long westward journey. During the Napoleonic Wars, when the English Channel was frequently unsafe for British shipping, the eastern route became still more popular.

Before the engineers of the nineteenth century gave Britain good networks of long-distance roads and railways, the easiest and fastest way to travel long distances was often by sea. As a result, Orkney felt less remote than some towns in the English Midlands, and there were opportunities for the lairds of eighteenth-century Orkney to make money from this passing trade.

One such family were the Honeymans. Robert Honeyman purchased the small island of Graemsay in 1699 and set up house at Clestrain. He was very successful, making lucrative land deals and acting as a money-lender. His son, Patrick, was also acquisitive, and wanted a house that reflected his increasing wealth and expanding estate. So in 1769 he built the present Hall of Clestrain in the fashionable style of the mid-eighteenth century. It was a statement that, financially, socially, and architecturally, his family had arrived.

But having arrived, they did not stay long on the island. Patrick's son, Sir William Honeyman, rose through the legal profession, eventually becoming a judge. By this time, the family were moving their power base to mainland Scotland, eventually settling in the Lanark area. The Hall became the home of the factor of the Honeymans' Orkney estate.

Although the stone stair treads still wind their way upwards, the banister shafts and rails have long disappeared.

A finely chiselled lintel and doorpost (right) show that the Honeyman family wanted to create an impression of quality and elegance.

Later the house was sold. It was still occupied in 1952, when a great storm ripped off the roof. The family moved out of the house and eventually it was used for keeping livestock. A number of concrete pig pens were installed in the basement, internal partition walls were removed, and some of the windows, especially those on the seaward side, were bricked up. The roof covering was replaced with asbestos.

So restoration will prove a major task. Research will be needed to find out about the original roof covering. This was slate, but could have come from Orkney, Scotland, or Wales. The chimneys will need rebuilding and researchers will try to answer the question of whether the house originally had a pediment and if so, whether this should be replaced. The walls will need repointing and rendering, while doors and sash windows will have to be replaced.

Inside, the restorers will need to remove the modern concrete pig pens and their floors. They may find the original stone flags beneath. On the main floor, marks on the walls show the positions of the original room partitions, because these were built as wood-framed stud walls, a method of construction that is common in Orkney houses. Upstairs no evidence survives to show where the internal walls were. The restorers will talk to people who remember the house, as well as using evidence from similar houses, to try to work out how the space should be divided. For decorative details such as cornices, mouldings, banisters, door frames, and skirting boards, restorers will be able to copy fragments that still survive in the house.

Walls green with lichen surround a window, partly blocked by boards, that retains some of its old glass.

So restoring the Hall of Clestrain will be a challenge, but one that is worthwhile. That the building is a very unusual survival of a Georgian laird's house and a key part of the island's history is reason enough to preserve it. But the house has additional importance because of its link with an important figure from Orkney's past, the explorer John Rae.

Born in 1813, John Rae was the son of the estate factor, another John, who lived in the house in this period. Young John trained as a surgeon in Edinburgh before joining the Hudson's Bay Company in Canada. Here he was both surgeon and explorer. Learning the arts of survival from the Canadian Inuit, he surveyed the coastline of northern Canada and was a leader of the Royal Navy land expedition which found the remains of Sir John Franklin's ill-starred attempt to locate the North-West Passage.

A combination of damp and the original colour of the stone makes for colourful interior walls around a blocked fireplace. There is much work to do here, but the structure itself is solid.

John Rae was a successful explorer who combined personal determination with a willingness to learn from the local people wherever he went. He also wrote extensively about the people, wildlife, and geography of the Arctic. Rae learned much of his skill with boats on the Orkney coast. On the shore not far from the Hall is the sail-house where Rae and his brothers stored their equipment, and the remains of the nousts, the boat-shaped hollows lined with stone, where they kept their craft. The Raes regularly took out one of the boats, and if they were not fishing for the family table, a favourite activity was to race the pilot boats of Stromness, often beating their rivals and leading visiting craft safely into harbour.

These links with the sea, which also provided the local lairds with much of their wealth, make the Hall of Clestrain an appropriate setting for the planned restoration project – an Orkney boat museum. To one side of the house is a large walled garden, and its high walls will mask a large new building that will contain a collection of around forty vessels from all over Orkney, dating from the early nineteenth century onwards. The boats include examples of many different local styles of yoles, the local craft of the coastal parishes of Orkney itself, together with skiffs, the indigenous craft of the island of Westray, and prams, the craft of North Ronaldsay. In addition there is a rare survival, a prehistoric oak log boat, perhaps the largest of its kind to come down to us. The building that houses these craft will be large, but will be masked from view by the old garden wall – only the new turf roof will be visible from outside.

It is planned to use the Hall itself to display smaller items from the collection. But each room will be restored in the Georgian style and at least one room will be furnished as the house would have been in its heyday. Steve Callaghan is enthusiastic about the way in which the boat museum will fit into the site. 'It's an ideal fit. Maritime history is especially appropriate to this site and the new building will blend in well. In addition there is the potential to employ an apprentice boat-builder to make boats in the traditional way and help keep the old crafts alive.' And Callaghan points out that there is plenty of local backing, and local knowledge, behind the project: 'Those involved in the company that is being set up to run the museum include a retired boat-builder and a former fisherman.' Orkney's maritime heritage, and its unique laird's house, seem to be in excellent hands.

Damp – and birds – have also affected the floorboards in the building's main rooms.

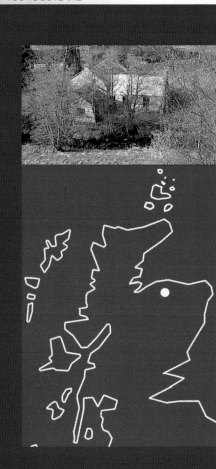

Knockando Wool Mill

From a distance it looks unassuming – a little cluster of low, grey buildings, roofed with corrugated iron, in a valley beside a stream. But Knockando is a unique survival of Scotland's industrial heritage, a small mill that has survived with its nineteenth-century cloth-making machinery still intact and working. There are few places anywhere in Europe quite like it.

In England and the border country, textile manufacture evolved as a number of specialised businesses. Hugh Jones, the mill's current owner, explained: 'One person would spin the yarn, another would weave it into cloth, and there would also be individual mills for processes such as fulling. Yarn and cloth would be carted from one mill to another and many different, often neighbouring, families would be involved in the business. But further north, single mill complexes developed that took on all of these processes, bringing in wool from the sheep in the fields next door and doing everything necessary to produce finished cloth.'

To begin with these mills were small enterprises, serving a local neighbourhood, so they became known as district mills. As the industrial revolution gathered pace in the nineteenth century and more and more machinery was introduced, some of these mills became quite large and grew into some of Scotland's most successful businesses, exporting their products far and wide. But some stayed small and eventually could not compete. Gradually, most of the district mills disappeared until only the one at Knockando remained.

Textile production has been going on here at least since 1784, when members of the Fraser family settled here and built the original mill. Throughout the nineteenth century the buildings were modified to take a series of new machines. First a carding machine was installed to comb the wool before spinning – Simon Fraser saw an opportunity to supply local hand-spinners with carded wool. Soon other machines were added, notably a spinning mule to mechanise the yarn production and finally a mechanical loom. At the same time the building grew, first with the addition of an extra stone building for the carding unit, then with the removal of inner partition walls to take larger machines like the spinning mule.

The area around the mill was also used by the family. In one nearby field are posts that formed part of the tenter frame, the structure on which woollen material was dried during the summer months. When poor weather prevented outdoor drying the winter drying shed, with its high-level drying poles (the origin of the phrase 'to be on tenterhooks'), was used.

Also nearby is the farm cottage, a two-room dwelling with a lean-to that may have been a dairy or larder. It was built in the early nineteenth century and was occupied by the mill owner and his family. Although it is modest, this house is well built with dressed stone. The masonry was covered with harling, and traces of the old lime render are still visible on the walls. The good-quality masonry and panelled doors of the cottage show that its original occupants had some status – the house is a cut above many rural buildings. Nearby is another house, dating from the late nineteenth century, and a small shop, which was kept open until 1975 for the sale of the blankets and tweeds made at the mill. The original shelves for the stock are still preserved inside.

The business was successful, and its blankets, tweeds, and knitting wools were sold as far afield as the Moray coast and Glenlivet.

Hugh Jones works at the loom at Knockando. His priority has been to keep this important and well-oiled machinery working, so that the unique district mill can continue to produce cloth.

Wooden walls, a corrugated metal roof, and flaking paint – it is an unassuming building, but it fits into the landscape and, most importantly, it works, just as it has done since the 1780s.

The Frasers, and the Smiths who took over in the 1860s, made a good living from the mill and the adjoining small farm. Duncan Stewart, the last member of the Smith family to work at the mill, was reducing his working hours when a group of new owners, including Hugh Jones, took over in 1976.

When Hugh Jones came to the mill he had no experience of textile manufacture and had to learn everything from scratch. It might seem a daunting prospect, but Hugh was unfazed. 'It wasn't that difficult,' he said. 'Most of the processes are straightforward to learn. The main thing is attention to detail, making sure everything on the machines is running properly, and learning to pre-empt problems.' And so Hugh learned how to keep the mill going, as the Frasers and Smiths had done before him. Hugh explained that their success was partly due to the fact that there was a small farm adjacent to the mill, offering the family another income stream. There were also personal reasons. 'When Duncan Stewart returned home from the war he was injured and could not farm as he had hoped. So he worked the mill and, together with his aunt Emma Smith, kept it going. When I arrived I learned a great deal from Duncan.'

Hugh designs and produces bespoke tweeds for local landowners, and for their gamekeepers who work on the estates on Speyside. In addition he makes cloth for the habits of the Benedictine monks at the nearby abbey at Pluscarden. Like Duncan before him, Hugh makes a living from this business, but there is little money left over for investment. 'So the buildings haven't had the restoration they deserve. These buildings are special and the work needs to be done properly. So I realised that the only route was to form a trust and to apply for public funding for a restoration, to release the full potential of the place.'

And that potential is considerable. Visitors will have the unique experience of seeing the nineteenth-century machinery working. The spinning and carding shed still contains the old carding set for combing out the wool, and the spinning mule, for producing woollen yarn, which dates from 1870. The two nineteenth-century looms are still functioning, both with chain-based control systems used to set the pattern of the cloth to be woven. So is the teasel gig, a machine that uses the seed heads of the teasel plant to fluff up the woollen cloth. The machine, with its

Machinery for carding still turns, as it did in the nineteenth century, although the old waterwheel no longer powers it.

mechanical drive and spiky teasel heads, seems to sum up a coming together of natural and man-made elements that is essential to this rural industry.

As part of the restoration project, some newer machinery may also be added, to help increase production, make the mill more sustainable, and ensure that funds are available for repairs in the future. And the adjacent eighteen acres of land could be farmed organically, providing another attraction for visitors.

One part of the old machinery that is not working is the old overshot waterwheel. The cast-iron wheel of 1860 still sits in its wheel pit lined with rubble masonry. But although the iron rims and spokes are in good condition, the wooden paddles have long since rotted away. One part of the proposed restoration is a plan to repair the wheel and get it turning again.

But the greatest challenge for the restorers is the work that is needed on the buildings themselves. Structural problems are clearly visible up in the warping attic, where the threads are strung for weaving. A sinking floor and collapsing beam show that the building is in a bad way.

Outside, there are clearly problems with the mill's roofs. A big dip in one roof is visible, caused by the weight of snow – repairs are needed soon to prevent further damage. There is also the question of the roof covering. To begin with, the mill was probably thatched. This material was later replaced with red pantiles. Finally, when these failed, they were replaced with corrugated iron. These changes show how keeping the mill working has always been the main priority.

Samples of golden woollen yarn glow in the bright light of the mill's large windows.

Rolls and hanks of yarn in a range of traditional colours, bobbins, and hand tools cover the mill's work surfaces, and visitors could be forgiven for thinking that this is industrial archaeology. In fact it is the equipment and stock-in-trade of a business, one that could bring economic success to the area if the restoration project went ahead.

And yet this very frugality has also kept the site largely unchanged. There has been no major expansion, no modern factory blocks made of steel and concrete, no state-of-the-art machinery. Lack of money has left the buildings in disrepair. But it has also saved them from demolition and has prevented important early machinery from being scrapped. Now it is time to break this cycle, to keep the machinery running still, but to make the major investment that the buildings deserve too.

Plenty of people should be attracted to the site – many tourists already visit the area to follow the Speyside whisky trail, and would be fascinated by a look at a very different industry. Others could come from further afield to see a process that has

RESTORATION Update Scotland
News from the first series

Those who care for Mavisbank House, the eighteenth-century Georgian mansion outside Edinburgh that reached the final in the last series, were impressed by the support they received after the programme – not only from local people, but from all over Britain. They have benefited from project-development funding from both the Heritage Lottery Fund and the Architectural Heritage Fund, and they are carrying out the various surveys necessary before their development plan can be finalised. Once the development plan is in place they will apply for funding for two main phases of work on the building and grounds. First, work will be done on the roof and exterior to make the house watertight; there will also be work on the grounds, which will be opened to the public. The second stage will be to restore the interior of the house.

After the receipt of grants from the Heritage Lottery Fund and Historic Scotland, together with many donations as the result of a local fund-raising campaign, restoration work is under way at Easthouse Croft on the Shetland island of West Burra. Those involved are very grateful to *Restoration* for giving the project the publicity it deserves, bringing the croft generous support from all over Britain. The future of the building – both as a community resource for West Burra and as a memorial to a way of life now vanished but once common all over northern Scotland – seems assured.

changed little in the past hundred years, and perhaps to buy some of the products in the restored mill shop.

In addition, there will be educational displays in the adjacent buildings, and some visitors may be inspired to learn more about the processes involved in textile working, to ensure that these special Scottish skills are passed on to the next generation. Hugh is aware of the potential, and hopes that, as well as saving the mill, the scheme could become a model for other threatened industrial buildings in Scotland. And then still more people will be grateful that yarn is still spun and cloth still woven at Knockando Wool Mill.

Fittings on the iron waterwheel (opposite) show the former positions of the wooden paddles. Work would be needed on both the paddles and the watercourse to get the wheel turning again.

The Glen o' Dee Sanatorium at Banchory also has good prospects. Due to movement in the housing market, the building has now become viable for residential use. The owners have re-marketed the building and have found a developer who can convert it in a way that is sensitive to its unique wooden structure.

As a result of the interest of Prince Charles, both the Landmark Trust and the Prince of Wales's Phoenix Trust are now discussing their possible involvement in Kinloch Castle on the Isle of Rum, the other Scottish finalist from the first series. The hope is to restore the castle so that it can provide accommodation for visitors to the island, to make the place accessible to people of different interests.

New plans at Nairn's Lino Factory in Kirkcaldy are to use part of the vast space as a much-needed storage facility for the collections of the museum and art gallery in Fife and for the local council archives. The other half of the building will be run by a community business trust, providing small units for local businesses and community groups. A new bid for funding from the Heritage Lottery Fund has been made.

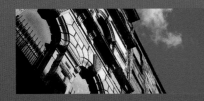

At Britannia Music Hall the roof covering has been replaced, ensuring that the precious interior is protected from the elements. The music hall has opened to its first paid audiences since its rediscovery, and custodians are now working on plans for further work on the building.

RESTORATION

NORTHERN IRELAND

Armagh Gaol ARMAGH

Lock-keeper's cottage NEWFORGE

The Playhouse LONDONDERRY

Some of the most beautiful countryside in the United Kingdom is to be found in Northern Ireland. The Mountains of Mourne in County Down and the stunning coastline around the Giant's Causeway in County Antrim are world-renowned; the waterside beauties of Lower Lough Erne and Lough Neagh are scarcely less striking. Ancient monasteries, ruined castles, and Georgian country houses make this countryside special for the lover of old buildings, too.

Northern Ireland also has notable towns and cities, some with an ancient history going back to the beginnings of Christianity in Ireland in the fifth century, some with their origins in the settlements created by incoming English and Scottish Protestants in the seventeenth century, others best known for their Victorian architecture. The three restoration candidates from Northern Ireland owe their existence to the Province's cities – one is in Armagh, another in Londonderry, and the third is near Belfast and was built as part of the effort to link Ireland's capital to other areas with a viable transport route.

Armagh is one of Ireland's oldest settlements. St Patrick came here and, according to tradition, made Armagh the headquarters of his Christian mission to Ireland. In 445 he

In the empty Armagh Gaol, an area around a stairway is thrown into deep shadow. Beyond, light from overhead windows catches rows of cell doors.

Render is cracking above the entrance to the Playhouse in Londonderry.

built his first church here and ever since then the place has been the heart of the Church in Ireland. Like many Irish towns, Armagh grew in the Georgian period, when the oval green space known as the Mall was lined with elegant houses. There are many buildings here that inspire affection in locals and visitors alike, but at one end of the Mall lies one of the least-loved buildings, Armagh Gaol. And yet it is a structure with so much to offer, if one can see beyond its sorry history, which is partly bound up with the Troubles and the policy of internment without trial that the British government pursued in Northern Ireland in the 1970s. The solution must be to look forward as well as remembering the past, to make new plans for the building that give the structure a new use while also incorporating some form of interpretation, so that future generations can still find out about its history.

The second candidate is at Newforge, near Northern Ireland's greatest city, Belfast. But Belfast, which became a great industrial and commercial centre in the nineteenth century, could not have prospered without proper transport links. One such link was the Lagan Navigation, an engineering project begun in the mid-eighteenth century which connected Belfast to Lough Neagh and which became a water-transport hub for much of Northern Ireland. One effect of this was to transform the rural scene, with the creation of numerous locks, accompanied by houses for the lock-keepers and often small, hump-backed bridges where the towpath crossed from one side of the water to the other. Places like the lock-keeper's cottage at

Newforge were once hives of activity, with boats waiting to pass through the lock and boatmen exchanging news with colleagues and acquaintances. Today, many have disappeared, but the group of lock, cottage, and bridge at Newforge remain, in need of restoration as a poignant reminder of this aspect of Ireland's social and economic history.

The third building is in Londonderry, another ancient city, where St Columba founded a monastery in the sixth century. This restoration candidate is a former school, now used as a community arts centre called the Playhouse. This building has also played its part in the varied religious history of the area, since it was the home of the first convent to be founded in Northern Ireland since the Reformation. It is a symbol of the good things religion has brought to the Province, as it was a place of education for around a century. Once again, in its role as an arts centre, the site is offering local people a chance to aspire to something above the mundane, to widen their horizons, and to tap the challenging, thought-provoking, and even spiritual experiences that art can bring. And these are benefits that every city needs.

Northern Ireland's restoration candidates are for the most part unglamorous working buildings. But they are certainly not dull. Each has much to tell us about the past of the Province, about the life of the people and the ability of their builders and architects. Restored, each could be effective in inspiring visitors and kindling local pride.

A corrugated metal roof covers the lock-keeper's cottage at Newforge. Though inappropriate visually, it at least protects the interior from the elements until restoration can take place.

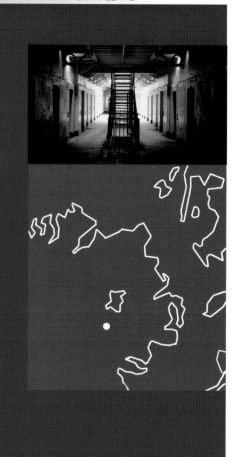

Armagh Gaol

In 1765 a new archbishop was appointed to the city of Armagh. His name was Richard Robinson, and under his influence the city was improved with major new building work by some of the most prominent architects of the period. The library and observatory both date from Robinson's time, as does the archbishop's own palace. Crime and punishment were tackled too, with a new courthouse and, eventually, a new prison.

Trevor Geary, a local man whose connection with the gaol goes back to his mother's time as a prison officer there in the 1950s, recalled a local tradition: 'There is a legend that a secret tunnel connects the gaol and the courthouse. Contractors discovered a void beneath the front of the gaol, but this may well have been part of a fuel cellar.' This is an example of the stories that the building attracts and the discoveries that have been made. Following the hints of another researcher, Trevor Geary discovered more underground remains, a number of 'dungeon cells': 'We removed a board and found a staircase going down. In the light from a ventilation opening and the glimmer from our torch we found cell doors.' Gas fittings suggested that these cells had been in use as recently as the 1960s or 1970s, but had lain forgotten since.

But the main gaol was begun in Robinson's time and built in two principal stages. In 1780 a block was built with four bays on either side of the entrance. This symmetrical block was designed to house male prisoners on one side and female inmates on the other. The architect was Thomas Cooley, a former carpenter who went on to design many buildings in Ireland, including Dublin's Royal Exchange and Four Courts. In 1819 the prison was criticised for being cramped, and an extra four-bay block and a further entrance bay were added, similar in style to the first, to create the fourteen-bay façade that can be seen today. It was arranged in three sections, housing women, male debtors, and male felons.

The fourteen bays of the façade are certainly impressive. The main material is a local stone known as conglomerate or 'pudding stone', so-called because it is a naturally occurring mixture of rounded stones in a cement-like body, looking rather like a cake mix. The entrance bays are picked out in

Inside the gaol's cell blocks many of the fittings, such as walkways, rails, and stairs, are made of metal. As well as being strong, these fittings, with their see-through construction, allowed warders a good line of sight.

Carved on a keystone, the date of this addition, 1816, is still just visible.

ashlar, stone that has been finely cut and smoothly finished, and the corner stones are rusticated, having deeply cut joints to give each block a monumental or massive appearance. Other details, such as the curved-headed windows with their keystones and the triangular pediments above the entrance bays, all add to the strong, monumental effect created by the building – it is a structure that radiates an impression of authority.

In addition to this main wing there were ancillary buildings, including the solitary block, treadwheel, and engine house. A two-storey building with a hipped roof housed the infirmary, and Armagh may have been the first prison in Britain to have such a facility for sick inmates. Further wings were added at intervals during the nineteenth century, until the gaol reached its final form in 1865.

The changes made over time show how prison reform brought better conditions. Hot-water pipes running through the building, for example, provided warmth, ensuring some comfort for the inmates during winter. The prisoners at Armagh were also lucky to have decent medical facilities in the nineteenth century. And there is evidence that the prison as a whole was run on humanitarian lines at this time. A report of 1888 praised the building and the way it was run. The account, by G. H. Bassett, also gives an idea of what the cell blocks looked like on the inside:

> The cells in both wards are kept in perfect condition, the most sensitive nose failing to perceive the faintest trace of that odour expected to be found associated with bolts and bars. There are two tiers of cells, one at each side of the ward. An iron gallery surrounds the upper tier and substantial rope netting covers the open space as a precaution against suicide. There are good bathing facilities and the sanitary arrangements throughout are excellent.

Armagh Gaol's interiors are functional (opposite), with plain doorways, signage painted in simple, clear lettering, and heavy cell doors with spy holes and speaking grilles.

Iron bars and heavily rusticated masonry create an architecture of authority for the exterior of the gaol.

In some ways, the architecture helped this cleanliness. The upstairs slate floors were long-lasting, fire-proof, and damp-proof. The slate's smooth surface could be washed down with ease. Another advanced feature was the good ventilation, which also carried away smells and helped to keep healthy fresh air flowing through the building. The prison was a cut above the previous gaol, a dark, crowded, and unsavoury structure beneath the Sessions Court in Market Street.

The authorities paid particular attention to the exercise yard. Originally this was a broad open space, but later it was subdivided with internal walls, fanning out and joining the perimeter wall to create more compact areas in which smaller groups of prisoners could exercise. Where the inner and outer walls joined, the perimeter wall was heightened with a semi-circle of stone, to make it harder to climb over.

But it was not all health, hygiene, and exercise. The prison was the scene of hangings after the archbishop moved the site of executions from Gallows Hill because it was overlooked by his palace. Executions continued throughout the nineteenth century. The last man to be hanged at Armagh Gaol was Joseph Fee, a 22-year-old man from County Monaghan who was convicted of murder and put to death in December 1904. The execution was carried out in a small shed built against the prison wall. The shed was whitewashed inside and, although it has long disappeared, whitewash remains on the prison wall where it stood.

Life could be tough for those who remained as inmates of Armagh Gaol. There was a strict punishment regime and this, too, was built into the architecture, in the dark, dungeon-like basement cells. Their cold stone floors and heavy doors studded with iron nails speak of a harsh fate for those who stepped out of line.

Another form of punishment was the treadwheel. Installed in 1832, it was in many ways the cruellest of all punishments. The great wheel could take sixteen prisoners at a time and they were required to take the eight-inch steps – which were only wide enough for their toes – at a rate of forty-eight per minute. Unsurprisingly, few could stand this for very long, and the usual routine was ten minutes on the wheel followed by five minutes' rest.

The treadwheel was totally unproductive. Its turning was not harnessed to provide power as it might have been. But by the time it was introduced, the idea of keeping prisoners busy with useful work was already established. This notion, too, was incorporated into the punishment regime, with wrongdoers put to heavy tasks such as breaking stones in the yard.

For much of the nineteenth century there were complaints about overcrowding in the prison. The 1846 Vagrants Acts put

There are a few decorative elements, notably in the ironwork – scroll-shaped brackets supporting the walkways and stair-risers made of metal circles.

an extra strain on accommodation, with beggars being thrown into gaol, and the famine exacerbated this problem. In 1847 there was an average count of ten prisoners in each cell and typhus, often known as 'gaol fever', was spreading rapidly. The 1865 extension helped to relieve this problem, bringing the prison back up to acceptable standards for the time.

The gaol served as a women's prison for much of the twentieth century. Most of the inmates were serving sentences for such crimes as theft and prostitution, and gave the authorities few problems. But things changed in the 1970s, when the Troubles were at their height. Prisoners found much to protest about, including government policies such as internment without trial, the removal of political-prisoner status, and the shooting by British troops of unarmed demonstrators in Londonderry on 30 January 1972, the day now known as Bloody Sunday. Inmates at Armagh also alleged that they were maltreated and subjected to degrading practices such as strip-searches and beatings.

In 1974 the discontent erupted. In a response to prisoner protests at the Maze Prison, west of Belfast, women in Armagh Gaol rioted and captured the prison governor and three prison officers. They gave up their hostages when they were assured by the Catholic chaplain that beatings at the Maze had been ended. But discontent continued, with hunger strikes and dirty protests, into the early 1980s. The gaol was finally closed in 1986.

Netting still stretches between the walkways. It was designed to catch anyone who threw themselves over – and to protect those below from objects falling or thrown from above.

Since then, the gaol has stood empty, its heavy stone walls challenging the authorities to come up with an acceptable use for a building that has harboured such a dark history and has inspired so much hatred. In the early 1990s there were plans to turn it into a shopping centre, but the city council responded to this inappropriate proposal by acquiring the building from its private owners. Since then they have made it secure, but the longer it remains empty, the more the structure will deteriorate.

Trevor Geary pointed out that substantial sums have recently been spent restoring the Mall, the courthouse, and other nearby buildings. The restoration of the gaol would be a fitting climax to the conservation of this historic part of the city. Current plans include converting part of the building to a museum explaining the history of the gaol. Guided tours of some of the Victorian cell blocks could also be provided and the usual visitor facilities installed. The gaol forecourt is already a dropping-off point for tourist coaches, so there would be a ready supply of visitors. The remainder of this large building could be converted to office space, to generate income and make the whole project sustainable. If a suitable tenant can be found for the office space, the gaol could play a much more positive role in the life of the city.

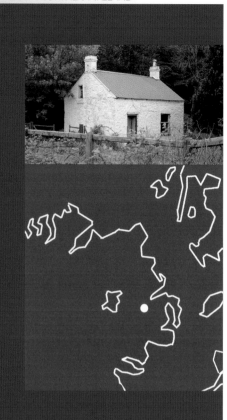

Lock-keeper's cottage

The most modest of buildings can tell us so much about how life was lived in the past, and for social and economic historians the humblest cottage can sum up the whole story of an area – from family life to industry. Such a building is the house at Newforge which was home to the keeper of number three lock on the Lagan Navigation.

The coming of the canals was a crucial part of the industrial revolution that swept across Britain and Ireland, beginning in the mid-eighteenth century. In 1753 coal was discovered on the Tyrone shore of Lough Neagh. It was a rich resource that could be used to power machinery in growing centres such as Dublin and Belfast. But how was it to be transported? The roads were poor, and even in good, level conditions a horse and cart could not manage to haul much more than a ton at a time. The answer was water transport, using the same horse to pull a barge loaded with as much as 70 or 80 tons of coal.

So the great expanse of water at Lough Neagh became the hub of a system of waterways. One of the most ambitious of these followed the course of the River Lagan, cutting off bends in places with new channels and making use of the natural river where it could be made navigable. The result was the Lagan Navigation, built, in the words of the 1753 Act of Parliament that authorised its construction, 'to increase the trade of Belfast and to furnish the several inhabitants of the towns of Belfast, Lisburn, Moira, and Hillsborough with many necessary materials of life in more plenty and at a cheaper rate than they can now be had'. By this time Dublin already had its Newry Canal, linking it to the coalfields. Belfast needed something similar if it was to keep pace with its rival.

May Blair, the historian of the Navigation, explained its developing role: 'The original intention had been to carry coal from Coalisland to Belfast, but the coal reserves were smaller than at first thought and the trade proved uneconomic. So most of the barges carried farm produce, such as potatoes and oats, from the countryside to Belfast. Lightermen were glad of any cargo going the other way, and often carried horse manure from Belfast to the farming country. They disliked the smell, but any cargo was better than no cargo.'

The canal is overgrown now, but the small stone bridge is a reminder of the effort that went into building it.

Close up the walls of the cottage can be seen to be made of a mixture of stone and brick, with a pierced stone below the window to provide extra ventilation.

Work began in 1756, under the engineer Thomas Omer, on the section linking Belfast and Lisburn. In 1763 the first boat, the *Lord Hertford*, laden with 45 tons of coal and timber and a band playing popular airs, made the passage. There was great enthusiasm for the new Navigation. Hundreds lined the banks to celebrate and many walked the towpath, discovering that the Navigation was a boon to walkers as well as those who worked on the water. But money was short and work soon halted on the remaining section to Lough Neagh. It was left to a private company, headed by the Marquis of Donegal, and an English engineer, Richard Owen, to complete the scheme, linking up with Lough Neagh at Ellis's Cut in 1794. This section was a challenge, with a rise through four locks and a descent to the lough through a further ten. Lock-keepers became some of the most vitally important people on the Lagan Navigation.

The Newforge lock-keeper's cottage is next to a lock and a hump-backed bridge on the original Belfast to Lisburn section of the Navigation. Although it is on this early section it is later than the canal itself, and was put up some time between 1827 and 1834. Built of random rubble with the occasional patch of

A broken window like this (opposite) can accelerate the cycle of decay, letting in rain, birds, plant seeds, and even vandals.

Both timber and masonry will need careful conservation.

handmade brick, it is now whitewashed, and its roof has been covered with metal sheeting since the original Bangor Blue tiles were stolen. At either end is a brick chimney stack – coal is one material that would have been in plentiful supply on the canal and the little house would have been well heated.

The interior is simple too, with an opening in the ground-floor ceiling to allow access to the bedrooms via a ladder. The only comfort comes from the fireplaces. There is no running water, no mains electricity, and until quite recently there was no connection to the sewer. It would not be a difficult job to recreate in the cottage the life lived by the lock-keeper and his family.

Outside, the cottage is close to two other typical features of the canal scene – the lock and bridge. The lock itself still retains its strong Silurian stone walls edged with dressed sandstone blocks. The lock gates are no longer there, but the recesses in the walls where they fitted are still visible. The bridge is made of similar stone to the lock walls, and is one of the few on the canal to survive in something close to its original condition.

Inside the cottage, the wallpaper, which must be thirty or forty years old, is peeling away from the walls.

The lock, built at a point where a length of canal cuts off a bend in the river, was one of 237 on the navigation, looked

after by eighteen lock-keepers. In the heyday of the canal it would have been a busy place. Lightermen queued up to pass through the lock, and it was the keeper's job to pass the barges through in the right order – there were often disputes about who had arrived at the lock first. The keeper had to manage the lock carefully, making sure that it did not overflow in times of flood, while conserving water when levels on the canal were low. The keeper at Newforge also had a weir to look after and, like many lock-keepers, probably kept goats, both for their milk and to crop the canalside grass. When the canal was quiet, there was also a garden to maintain. When wages were low the garden was a useful perk, supplying the family with vegetables. Coal could be another perk, the gift of lightermen who expected favourable treatment and a swift passage through the lock in return.

The barges were businesslike craft built of pitch pine. Most were horse-drawn and the early craft also carried sails to get them across the wide waters of Lough Neagh, although later the Navigation company provided tugs to do this job. At a lock, the lightermen were expected to defer to the lock-keeper and obey his instructions. There are records of fines being imposed on boatmen who passed through a lock when the keeper was

A closer look at the wallpaper reveals the sort of archaeology typical of *Restoration* – an older, more delicately patterned, paper beneath.

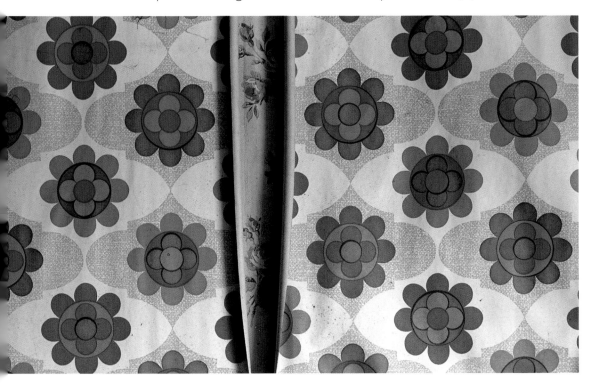

Another interior detail shows still older decorative finishes: peeling plaster and tongue-and-groove boards that would still look well if they were sensitively repaired and painted.

not present. They were also expected to handle their craft with care, making sure that their lighter did not hit one of the lock gates or collide with the lock walls.

Provided that speed was not important, since a horse could only pull a barge at a walking pace, the canal was an efficient way to carry cargo. Many canals prospered, bringing a good income in tolls to their shareholders and providing a vital service for shops and factories. The Lagan Navigation, too, did well, especially at the end of the nineteenth century. Barges carried all manner of goods – sand, timber, bricks, grain, and of course coal. But there was a problem with the Lagan Navigation – a lack of water on the upper canal stretches and flooding lower down in the river. It meant that those lock-keepers who had control of a weir had to be especially vigilant. This difficulty sometimes slowed the traffic on the canal to a standstill, especially when floods created dangerous situations with collapsed banks and carried sand and gravel into the waterway. As May Blair puts it in her book *Once Upon the Lagan*, 'the canal for some reason was allowed to fall into such disrepair that it was said that a ship could get to the West Indies and back faster than it took for a canal boat to do the round trip to Lough Neagh'.

But the canal carried on. Repairs were undertaken in the 1820s and there followed several decades of faster journey times and

A close look at the walls reveals how the builders filled the gaps between the larger stones with a mixture of small stones and mortar.

better traffic. But by the 1930s the competition was much stiffer, as swifter road and rail carriers took much of the Navigation's traffic. After World War II, very few barges were using the Navigation and in 1958 the Lagan Navigation Company was officially dissolved and the route closed. By this time the lock-keeper was George Kilpatrick, a man from a family of lock-keepers who had done the job at Newforge since 1922. He and his wife had brought up no fewer than ten children in the little house. When the canal closed, George bought the house and his youngest son lived there until he died in 1993. His sister inherited the house and sold it to the local council in the hope that public access would be allowed to a building that was much loved in the area.

In the nineteenth and early twentieth centuries the Lagan Navigation played a vital role in the transport network in Ulster. It is difficult to find some of the locks now, but the one at Newforge, with its cottage and bridge, is still a landmark. It offers a special opportunity for restoration and for facilities to explain the story of the canal, its construction, and the life and work of those who lived beside it. It is a fascinating aspect of Northern Irish history that should not be allowed to perish.

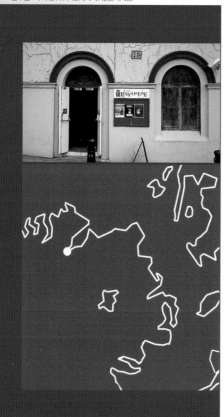

The Playhouse

The sense of place, the complex of emotions and associations that give a location its special character, is influenced by many factors such as the appearance of the landscape and the age and style of the buildings found there. But it is also to do with history, the way in which a place or a building has been used over the centuries and the role it has played in the wider community. The building now known as the Playhouse in the centre of the city of Londonderry is a case in point.

When community arts worker Pauline Ross came here to open the Playhouse in 1992, the building had already been a focus of community learning and education for more than a hundred years. Pauline immediately saw the building's potential as a community arts centre. 'The building has a great emotional warmth about it,' she explained. 'And the wooden panelling means that actors and musicians love the acoustics. Even young children can make themselves heard from the stage with ease.'

The site is one of Londonderry's oldest, and it is hard by the city walls in Artillery Street and nearby Pump Street. In the early nineteenth century it housed a hotel, the King's Arms, but in 1840 this was bought on behalf of the city's Roman Catholic bishop – on his behalf because Catholics were not allowed to purchase property within the city walls. This allowed the Church to establish a convent, the first in Northern Ireland since the Reformation. They also set up a small private school in Pump Street, the income from which paid the nuns' living expenses and funded charitable works. Later, they acquired more land in Artillery Street and built larger school premises to create St Mary's School, partly in response to the extra demand for places created by the 1880 Education Act, which ensured education for all children up to ten years old. Further expansion, to create St Joseph's School, took place a few years later to meet further demand.

By the early twentieth century, the buildings on Artillery Street had taken their present form, from the outside at least. The two adjoining structures differ quite markedly from one another. St Mary's, on the left-hand side as one looks at the building from the street, has a rather plain façade, which is now rendered and painted white. The round-headed windows and

doorway on the ground floor give it a certain elegance, but the sash windows above create the familiar impression given by terraced buildings in towns all over Ireland. In fact, though, these windows were unusual at the time. When they were installed they were the first sash windows in Derry. So a feature that now looks rather ordinary was extraordinary when it was new.

The adjoining St Joseph's building, though, still looks extraordinary. Its frontage clearly suggests that it was designed to make a big impression. Although still only a three-storey building, it is much taller than its neighbour because the two lower storeys have high ceilings and windows. These large windows are notable for their size alone, but they are made even more so by being surrounded with elaborate cement rendering that creates a whole vocabulary of classical details. All the ground-floor windows are topped with triangular pediments and framed by mouldings that look like massive blocks of masonry – the technique known as rustication, favoured by classical architects all over Europe. The even larger first-floor windows have rusticated arches and between each is

Rails of costumes are a reminder that this is very much a building in continuous and lively use.

Triangular pediments and other classical details give this part of the façade an air of grandeur.

a false column, topped with an elegant capital with the spiral volute design of the Ionic order. Above the doorway are even more prominent Ionic columns and capitals, supporting a feature known as a broken pediment – a pediment that breaks off in the middle, in this case to accommodate the lower portion of the window above.

The visual grandeur of this frontage takes the breath away, but a closer look hints that the splendour is more than skin deep. The large windows are there not just to look impressive but to ensure that the interiors are flooded with light. And up on the roof are three ventilation cowls, a reminder that clean air was an important priority in Victorian building – clean air meant a healthy interior, as important as ever in a period when millions died from influenza and tuberculosis.

This impressive structure was the brainchild of a prominent Derry architect, Edward Toye. He was very active in the city, working on numerous churches including the completion of St

Inside, the combination of materials is typical of a school of the early twentieth century, but the bright paint finishes add extra dazzle in keeping with the building's current role as a community arts centre.

Eugene's Cathedral, on school projects, and on other public buildings. He also designed banks in Derry, Cavan, and Ballybofey. St Joseph's shows how he could make his mark, even in a cramped site on a city street.

Behind the façade, the building was impressive in a different way. Practical features included a glass-covered veranda to connect the convent with the school. Glass was also much used inside, with many of the interior walls almost half glass, so that the natural light admitted by the generous windows could stream from one room to the next. Among the rooms treated in this way were the domestic-science room, in which dressers filled with rows of dishes and plates lined the wall beneath the glazing, and the boarders' refectory, where pupils sat on rows of bentwood chairs at a long table. Another important room was the science laboratory, with its state-of-the-art equipment — clearly a well-rounded education was the aim in this impressive building. The big windows still let the light flood in, and more so now that many of the interior walls have been removed.

In the entrance way to the arts centre, worn wooden flooring blocks look almost like bricks — and are just as tough.

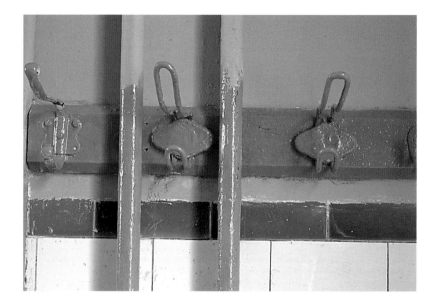

Metal pegs and two-colour tiling provide more memories of the building's original purpose as a school.

Education continued on the site for much of the twentieth century, at different levels and at different times under the auspices of the convent and state-school systems. The buildings served as a school until the 1980s, when St Joseph's was used for a while by the Derry Diocese for their work with the young unemployed. Finally, in 1986, it seemed that St Joseph's had outlived its usefulness, and an application was made to demolish the building. This was refused, and the buildings were bought by local investor Joe Mulheron.

A few years later, Pauline Ross was planning a new arts initiative. Her vision was to create a centre where all the arts would be made accessible to all the people of Londonderry. Once she had secured some initial funding she started to look for a building. A chance meeting put her in touch with Joe Mulheron, and the Playhouse was established on Artillery Street.

In over a decade the Playhouse has developed to play a major part in the life of the city. It has a gallery and other facilities for the visual arts on the ground floor, a theatre, green room, and rehearsal space on the first floor, and a dance studio on the second floor. The building provides a base for various theatre companies, dance groups, and other arts organisations. To achieve these facilities, the building has been altered slightly internally. Pauline Ross explained, 'We had to do very little to the building. We wanted to alter it as little as possible, so as not to lose the soul of the building. The main task was to take out

The encrusted and corroding pipework looks picturesque. But defective pipes can cause damage, and damp is one of the problems that needs to be addressed at the Playhouse.

some of the partition walls between the old classrooms, which we were able to do easily ourselves.'

The good work of the Playhouse has been rewarded with grants, but there have been difficult times financially. It is hard for an organisation living from one grant application to the next to find funds to restore buildings that are over a hundred years old. And they would like to expand by acquiring the old convent on Pump Street to help them to create additional facilities, such as spaces for artists in residence. At the moment some of these extra facilities are housed in temporary structures in the central courtyard.

The buildings on Artillery Street and Pump Street have played a very important role in the history of Derry. The sisters' work brought immense benefits to the Catholic population in the city – help to the poor, relief to the sick, and, of course, education to countless young people. Now the buildings are serving the city again, bringing the experience of the arts to a huge range of people in the community. Locals realise this and there is great support in the city for the Playhouse, which has also received funding over the years from bodies as diverse as the Arts Council and Children in Need.

And so the Playhouse has kept going, but it does not have the resources needed to restore the building. It is now reaching crisis point. Plants are growing in the masonry next to the

Sister Aloysius is one of the few artists today to specialise in the painting of icons. Both traditional and contemporary art come together at the Playhouse – appropriately enough in a city with a long history and a lively present.

pediment above the entrance. There are cracks in the walls. Water is getting into the building. The roof and guttering need attention soon if the rain is not to cause more damage. The Playhouse also needs better heating and disabled access. But Pauline Ross and her colleagues are aware of the need for a light touch, to retain the building's personality and maintain the impression that they are working in an old building that simply feels 'right' for its users. They want to restore it without turning the place into a palace of art – as the theatre director David Grant told Pauline, 'Don't lose your non-preciousness.' It is a good motto, as they plan their restoration of this city landmark while continuing their work with the people of Londonderry, fostering optimism and unity through art and inspiration.

RESTORATION Update Northern Ireland News from the first series

The Sion Mills Building Preservation Trust is pleased to be proceeding with the first phase of the project to restore the enormous Herdmans Mills site, for which funding has been in place for some time now. Work is also under way on creating business plans and master plans for the rest of the scheme, so that further fund-raising can take place. The Northern Ireland government is firmly behind the project, as are the local authority and supporters far and wide, many of whom have got to know about the site as a result of its coverage on *Restoration*. The next stage will be an application to the Heritage Lottery Fund. Trustees are confident that the full restoration will eventually go ahead.

A higher profile and increased visitor numbers have been reported at Lissan House, with interest coming from all over the UK and still farther afield. Funding is in place from the Heritage Lottery Fund to undertake audience, access, and conservation plans and this planning stage will be followed by an application to the HLF for major funding towards the house's refurbishment. Meanwhile, the Friends of Lissan Trust is making further applications to other funders to make up the shortfall. Trustees report that the coverage of Lissan House on *Restoration* has invigorated them and encouraged them to renew their efforts to secure the future of the house.

At the Crescent Arts Centre there is good news – that the centre is to receive a major contribution towards the building's refurbishment through an Arts Council grant. This should open the door to funding from other sources too, and talks about this and applications are under way. Again the response to *Restoration* has been very positive, and support in Belfast – and beyond – for this important community arts centre remains as strong as ever. When restoration begins, the plan is to phase the work so that the centre's activities can continue with a minimum of interruption. Meanwhile the profile of the centre was placed firmly behind the fate of all buildings at risk in Northern Ireland when the Buildings at Risk Online Database for the Province was launched at the Crescent in January 2004.

RESTORATION

What you can do to help

Perhaps there is a building near you that is at risk of collapse or decay. What can you do to help? A book like this can only suggest some starting points, and direct the reader towards further sources of information. Fortunately, our architectural heritage is so rich, and yet is in such need, that many organisations have sprung up to support and provide information for people caring for buildings at risk. The names and addresses of some of these organisations are given on pages 224–225. Below are a few hints about how to begin.

Peeling ceiling at the Old Grammar School.

First . . .

There are several different starting points. One approach is to ask one of the charities that exists to save and conserve old buildings whether it might take the building on. If you are able to persuade them, you will have the satisfaction of knowing at least that you started the process going, and that the building is in good hands. But you may want to get more involved than this. If you have the money – and a great deal of time and commitment – you may be able to buy the building and restore it yourself.

For most people, though, the most attractive option lies somewhere in between these two. They want to get involved, but cannot afford the money or the risk in taking the whole project on themselves. For this group – and it includes the custodians of most of the buildings featured in *Restoration* – the solution is often to set up a charity, known as a Building Preservation Trust (BPT), to acquire and restore the building.

There are many advantages to setting up a BPT. For example, BPTs are eligible for grant aid that is not available to individuals or commercial companies, they are set up as limited companies so that the personal risk to individual members is reduced, they are relatively straightforward to set up because a standard BPT 'template' exists, and they can benefit from specialist advice from certain expert organisations, such as the Architectural Heritage Fund (AHF) and the Association of Building Preservation Trusts. On the other hand, membership of a BPT also entails obligations, especially to conform with the laws that govern charities in the UK.

Facts

For many buildings, a BPT formed by a group of committed enthusiasts is the ideal solution. But before you begin to form a trust, you need to start out on the first step of any restoration project – research. Find out everything you can about your building. You need to look into every conceivable area.

You will need to be aware of your building's history. How old is it? Who built it? How has it developed over the years? Do old documents or plans exist? What roles has it played in the local community? How was the building used and has its use changed over the years?

You will want to come to terms with its architecture and structure. What materials is it built out of? Was there an architect and, if so, who? What specialist skills will be needed to restore it? What are the structural problems and how urgent are the solutions? Is there a safety issue?

And you will need to know how the planning authorities regard your building. Is it listed? Is it in a conservation area? Is it on a buildings at risk register?

These are just some of the questions you will need to address. Of course, some of them will be easy to answer, others less so. But looking at the building in this way will help you begin to see what sort of structure you are taking on, what its problems are, and how they might be solved. And as you ask around, you will start to discover others who know the building, are interested in its fate, and may be able to join you in your efforts to save it.

Warning sign at Castle House.

You will soon realise that there are plenty of people prepared to give you advice, and a successful restoration project will be a well-advised one. Specialist societies such as the Georgian Group, the Victorian Society, and the Twentieth Century Society provide excellent starting points if your building falls within their remit. So do the AHF, the Association of Building Preservation Trusts, and the Civic Trust. Other groups, such as the Society for the Protection of Ancient Buildings, run courses on various aspects of conservation and restoration. And do not forget local planners, the council officers who will need to be consulted when you make your plans for restoration. They have unique knowledge, both of the planning system and of local buildings, and it is wise to start talking to them early on in the process.

Funding

A lot of the work of restoring an old building comes down to raising money. Fortunately there are numerous sources of money available to charitable trusts that are specifically designed to fund restoration or heritage projects. The Heritage Lottery Fund is one well-known funder. The AHF advises on other sources. But no funder will give away public money without asking a lot of pertinent questions. They will want to know exactly what is special about your building – why they should give money to it rather than to some other structure that is equally at risk. They will want to know that your project is going to benefit the public or the community in some way. It is not enough for the building itself to be a 'good cause' – projects that provide some community, educational, social, or similar benefit will stand a much greater chance of success. Funders will almost certainly want you to match their money with an equal or greater amount from other sources. And they will want to know that you have done all the relevant studies – from reports on the building's structural state to conservation studies, from descriptions of end-use to demonstrations that you will make the building accessible to the disabled – before they will consider making a grant. So you must talk to the funders, and to people who understand the funding process, and make sure you are asking the right body in the right way.

Meanwhile, to get things going and to start finding the matching funds, you will need to start your own money-raising campaign. The *Restoration* pack, available via the BBC website, is full of ideas on how to raise money locally, from organising raffles and parties to schemes that offer the chance of sponsoring a brick or a plank of the restored building. You also need to network. Talk to local businesses and get everyone involved. Not everyone will be able to give you cash donations, but you may get offers of help in kind, and this can be just as valuable.

It is a long haul. You will need to draw on every contact and try every publicity-seeking idea, from articles in the local paper to events that make a splash. Again, the *Restoration* pack has valuable advice about how to contact the press and how to give them the information they need in order to write stories about your cause.

Future

Every building was built for a reason. Sometimes, buildings decay because they are no longer usable for their original function. So when you restore a building you need to ask what it will be used for in the future. And that use has to be sustainable. In other words, the newly restored building must supply a real need, preferably one that generates at least enough income to pay the repair bills in the future. Otherwise you could be back to square one in ten or twenty years' time.

Decaying timbers at Castle House.

Sometimes the end use is obvious. Griff Rhys Jones has been the leading light in the successful campaign to restore the Hackney Empire. Hackney needs its theatre, so the building's end-use is obvious. But sometimes it is not so straightforward. How do you use a redundant church or abandoned factory? It is not usually enough to turn it into a museum or a tourist attraction, though this can be a solution. A mixed use, for example letting part of the building as flats or offices and opening the remainder to the public, may make better sense – provided, of course, that this can be achieved without destroying what is historically important about the building.

This is why in the two series of *Restoration* many of the proposals for the buildings involve a mix of uses. But it is not just a ruse to keep a project afloat. A vibrant, restored mixed-use building can be a real asset to a community, restoring local pride and spirit as well as bricks and lime mortar.

And that is the point. It is an immensely valuable thing to bring a beautiful old building back to life, so that everyone can appreciate its beauty again. But to rekindle pride, to restore the special local feel of a place, to be part of an effort that will enhance the life of your community – and will do so for years to come – that is something that makes the campaigning, the waiting, the sheer hard work deeply fulfilling.

RESTORATION Useful addresses

Ancient Monuments Society
St Anne's Vestry Hall
2 Church Entry
London EC4V 5HB
020 7236 3934
www.ancientmonumentssociety.org.uk

Architects Accredited in Building
Conservation
11 Oakfield Road
Poynton
Cheshire SK12 1AR
01625 871458
www.aabc-register.co.uk

Architectural Heritage Fund (AHF)
Clareville House
26–27 Oxendon Street
London SW1Y 4EL
020 7925 0199
www.ahfund.org.uk

Association of Building Preservation Trusts
Clareville House
26–27 Oxendon Street
London SW1Y 4EL
020 7930 1629
www.heritage.co.uk/bpt

Building Conservation Directory
Cathedral Communications
High Street
Tisbury
Wiltshire SP3 6HA
01747 871717
www.buildingconservation.com

Cadw
Crown Building
Cathays Park
Cardiff CF1 3NQ
01222 500200
www.cadw.wales.gov.uk

Civic Trust
259–269 Old Marylebone Road
London NW1 5RA
020 7170 4299
www.civictrust.org.uk

English Heritage
23 Savile Row
London W1X 1AB
020 7973 3000
www.english-heritage.org.uk

Georgian Group
6 Fitzroy Square
London W1T 5DX
020 7529 8920
www.georgiangroup.org.uk

Historic Scotland
Longmore House
Salisbury Place
Edinburgh EH9 1SH
0131 668 8600
www.historic-scotland.gov.uk

Institute of Historic Building
Conservation (IHBC)
Jubilee House
High Street
Tisbury
Wiltshire SP3 6HA
01747 873133
www.ihbc.org.uk

National Trust
36 Queen Anne's Gate
London SW1H 9AS
0870 609 5380
www.nationaltrust.org.uk

National Trust for Scotland
Wemyss House
28 Charlotte Square
Edinburgh EH2 4ET
0131 243 9300
www.nts.org.uk

Royal Institute of British Architects (RIBA)
66 Portland Place
London W1B 1AD
020 7580 5533
www.riba.org

Royal Institute of Structural Engineers
11 Upper Belgrave Street
London SW1X 8BH
020 7235 4535
www.istructe.org.uk

Royal Institution of Chartered Surveyors
Surveyor Court
Westwood Way
Coventry CV4 8JE
0870 333 1600
www.rics.org

SAVE Britain's Heritage
77 Cowcross Street
London EC1M 6BP
020 7253 3500
www.savebritainsheritage.org

Society for the Protection of Ancient
Buildings (SPAB)
37 Spital Square
London E1 6DY
020 7377 1644
www.spab.org.uk

Scottish Civic Trust
Tobacco Merchant's House
42 Miller Street
Glasgow G1 1DT
www.scotnet.co.uk/sct

Twentieth Century Society
70 Cowcross Street
London EC1M 6EJ
020 7250 3857
www.c20society.demon.co.uk

Ulster Architectural Heritage Society
66 Donegal Pass
Belfast BT7 1BU
01232 550213
www.uahs.co.uk

University of York Centre for
Conservation
Department of Archaeology
The King's Manor
York YO1 7EP
01904 433901
www.york.ac.uk/depts/arch

Victorian Society
1 Priory Gardens
Bedford Park
London W4 1TT
020 8994 1019
www.victorian-society.org.uk

Weald and Downland Open Air Museum
Singleton
Chichester PO18 0EU
01243 811363
www.wealddown.co.uk

West Dean College
West Dean
Chichester PO18 0QZ
www.westdean.org.uk

RESTORATION Checklist of restoration candidates

THE SOUTH WEST

Sherborne House
(Open to the public.)
Newland
Sherborne
Dorset
DT9 3JG
01935 816426

South Caradon Mine
(Not open to the public. Private land.)
Caradon Hill
Minions
Bodmin Moor
Cornwall

Castle House
(Not open to the public. View from the exterior.)
Queen Street
Bridgwater
Somerset
TA6 3DA

THE SOUTH EAST

The Archbishop's Palace
(Not open to the public. Private land.)
Market Place
Charing
Kent

Strawberry Hill
(Open on Sundays, Easter to October. For opening times call 020 8240 4224.)
Waldegrave Road
Twickenham
TW1 4SX

Severndroog Castle.
(Not open to the Public. View from the exterior. In a public park.)
Shooter's Hill
Greenwich
London
SE18

THE MIDLANDS AND EAST ANGLIA

Newstead Abbey
(Open to the public.)
Newstead Abbey Park
Ravenshead
Nottinghamshire
NG15 8GE
01623 455912

The Old Grammar School and Saracen's Head
(Not open to the public. View from the exterior.)
Pershore Road
King's Norton
Birmingham
B30 3EX

Bawdsey Radar Station
(Not open to the public. Private land.)
Bawdsey Manor
Bawdsey
Suffolk

THE NORTH

Sheffield Manor Lodge
(Open to the public.)
115 Manor Lane
Sheffield
S2 1UH
0114 276 2828

Gayle Mill
(Not open to the public.)
Near Hawes
Yorkshire

Lion Salt Works
(Open to the public.)
Ollershaw Lane
Marston
Northwich
Cheshire
CW9 6ES
01606 41823

WALES

Cardigan Castle
(Not open to the public.)
Cardigan
Ceredigion
West Wales
SA43 1JA

Llanfyllin Union Workhouse
(Not open to the public.)
Llanfyllin
Powys
SY22 5LD

Celynen Workingmen's Institute and Memorial Hall
(Open to the public.)
High Street
Newbridge
Gwent
South Wales
NP11 4FH
01495 243252

SCOTLAND

Portencross Castle
(Not open to the public. View from the exterior.)
Portencross
West Kilbride

Hall of Clestrain
(Not open to the public. Private land.)
Orphir
Orkney
KW17 2RD

Knockando Wool Mill
(Not open to the public. Private land.)
Knockando
Morayshire
AB 387RP

NORTHERN IRELAND

Armagh Gaol
(Not open to the public. View from the exterior.)
Gaol Square
Armagh
BT60 1AQ

The lock-keeper's cottage
(Not open to the public. View from the exterior.)
117 Milltown Road
Newforge
Belfast
BT8 4XP

The Playhouse.
(Open to the public.)
5 –7 Artillery Street
Londonderry
BT48 6RG
028 7126 8027

Index

Main entries are shown in bold: further
illustrations outside of these pages are
shown in *italic*.